THE

HANDBOOK

OF **NATURAL**

PLANT DYES

SASHA DUERR

The

HANDBOOK
OF NATURAL
PLANT DYES

PERSONALIZE YOUR CRAFT *with* ORGANIC COLORS
from ACORNS, BLACKBERRIES, COFFEE, *and*
OTHER EVERYDAY INGREDIENTS

TO MY COLORFUL
FAMILY TREE

FRONTISPIECE: *These yarns have been dyed with kitchen waste: coffee, blackberries, onionskins, and avocado rinds.*
OPPOSITE: *Japanese maple leaf dye bath smells a bit like hibiscus when the color is first being extracted.*
PAGE 6: *Heirloom plants grown in healthy soil thrive in my uncle's biodynamic garden.*

Photograph credits are on page 161.

Published in 2010 by Timber Press, Inc.

The Haseltine Building
133 S.W. Second Avenue, Suite 450
Portland, Oregon 97204-3527
www.timberpress.com

2 The Quadrant
135 Salusbury Road
London NW6 6RJ
www.timberpress.co.uk

Printed in China

Library of Congress Cataloging-in-Publication Data
Duerr, Sasha.
    The handbook of natural plant dyes : personalize your craft with organic colors from acorns, blackberries, coffee, and other everyday ingredients / Sasha Duerr
        p. cm.
    Includes bibliographical references and index.
    ISBN 978-1-60469-071-2
    1. Dyes and dyeing—Textile fibers. 2. Dyes and dyeing, Domestic. 3. Dye plants. I. Title.
    TT854.3.D92 2010
    667'.3—dc22
                                        2010013697

A catalog record for this book is also available from the British Library.

THE AIM OF ALL ORGANIC PRACTICES—
PERMACULTURE, BIODYNAMICS, NATURAL FARMING
—IS NOT JUST TO REDUCE AND IDEALLY TO
ELIMINATE THE USE OF TOXIC CHEMICALS THAT
ARE HARMFUL TO HUMANS, ANIMALS, PLANTS
AND THE PLANET, BUT TO UNDERSTAND THE
PROCESSES OF NATURE IN ORDER TO PARTICIPATE,
RATHER THAN TO INTERFERE.

—Jacqueline Walker, from *Hibiscus*

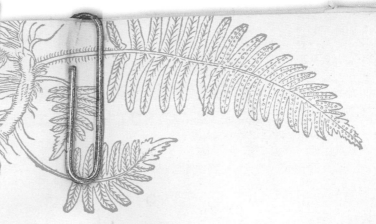

Introduction

Dyeing with Plants

Cultivating color, by growing beautiful plants in your garden and making your own botanical dyes, can be a wondrous experience. Whether you are an artist, a crafter, or a novice, you can easily learn how to create natural dyes from plants you have gathered or grown yourself. Soaking plant materials in water to make dye is as simple as making tea. Everyday plants like blackberries, carrots, and turmeric, to name just a few, can create an inspiring color palette. By following the simple instructions in this book, you can dye yarn, fabric, a sweater, a dress, or a tablecloth with botanical materials and transform an object into a work of art.

Creating color from plants is much like cooking: alchemy is everything.

WHY PLANT DYES?

Plant-based dyes offer colors that are unusual, varied, and vibrant.
Colors yielded by plant materials have a rich complexity that synthetic dyes cannot achieve.

Natural dyes harmonize with each other in a way that only botanical colors can. A natural dye, a red for example, will include hints of blue and yellow, whereas a chemically produced red dye contains only a single red pigment, making the color less complex. Even mixing synthetic dyes can rarely if ever achieve the range of shades that natural dyes possess.

When you work with organic botanical color sources, you are literally working with living color. The unique qualities of naturally dyed textiles can often make the color vibrate or glow, which is truly magical. In a hank of gray yarn, one person may see purple tones and another person may see blues. Natural dyes are sometimes less colorfast over time than synthetic dyes, but their richness is always inspiring.

Plant-based dyes offer an ecologically friendly alternative to synthetic dyes because they come from plants, which can be renewable nontoxic resources and are biodegradable. Botanical dyes love many types of natural fibers from plants and animals, and bond to them readily. Natural dyes take especially well to natural fibers such as wool, silk, linen, and cotton. When choosing items to dye, however, you aren't limited to textiles and fabrics, but can dye yarn for knitting, paper, shoes, lamp shades, rugs, and even your hair! And you can also dye the surfaces of many other objects, like wood beads, shells, and leather.

The bold yellow flowers of sour grass (Bermuda buttercup) are a first sign of spring in many regions. Children love to chew on the end of the stalks for their sour taste.

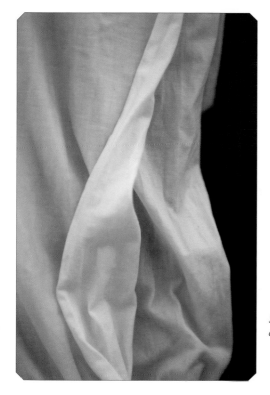

Sour grass flowers collected fresh from the garden create this beautiful yellow-green.

Gathering wild plant material from the sidewalks or vacant lots of your community is a good way to get acquainted with dye-producing botanical sources. Japanese maple leaves from the sidewalk will create gorgeous pinks to deep grays and blues; fennel, which grows widely as a weed, creates bright yellows and greens. Even plants commonly considered useless weeds create some of the most striking colors: sour grass makes bright yellows on all types of natural fibers. Fruit and nut trees also create beautiful colors: fig leaves make bright yellow and green, black walnut hulls make a rich brown, and the bark of the crabapple tree yields warm tones of pink to orange. Dye plants you can grow in your garden range from onions, whose skin produces bright yellows, greens, and orange-pinks, to red cabbage, which creates shades from lavender to deep blue, to herbs like mint, which creates tans to teal-greens.

You can sometimes achieve even more impressive ranges of color when using a mordant in the dyeing process. A mordant is a metallic agent used in the dyeing process that helps color chemically bind to the fiber. Some dyes will not take to fiber without a mordant, so it's important to check dye and project instructions carefully to see if a mordant is needed. However, many plants have the chemistry to allow vibrant color to bond with fiber, and those are particularly fascinating to work with. In my own exploration of color, I like to work with nontoxic natural dyes and mordants that are not harmful to the dyer or the environment. Some metallic mordants can contain toxic substances, so it's important to do your research and know your materials. With proper usage, the dyes and mordants in this book are safe to work with.

GROWING UP WITH NATURE

I spent my first years in Maine, during the back-to-the-land movement. We lived on an organic Christmas tree farm. When I was eight, we moved to Hawaii and lived near a volcanic black sand beach. I spent most of my childhood outdoors.

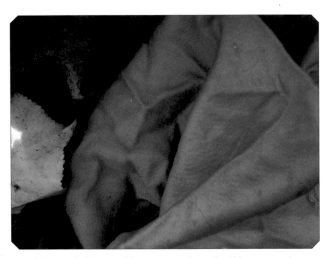

Color can be harvested from your garden or local farmers market. Red cabbage created this brilliant blue-purple.

Colors and textures surrounded me: bright white snow, deep brown mud, cerulean blue waters, pink granite rocks, and porous black lava. Avocados as big as my hand would drop from trees onto jungle pathways, aloe could be cut from bushes in our neighborhood to heal the wounds from falling off my bike. In both Maine and Hawaii, natural materials were always present to experiment with. I made houses out of sticks and moss, I played in bamboo forests, and I made my own shampoo out of hibiscus flowers. As a young child, I began to realize that there was a symbiosis between culture and nature. That one could not function without the other. That there was practical purpose and creative opportunity in knowing the plants that grow around you.

In college I studied painting, and the industrial oil-based paints and pigments I was using to do my work made me feel sick from the toxins they contained. Because I had grown up in a do-it-yourself culture and with a close connection to nature, I instinctively knew that creating beauty did not need to make you sick. Unfortunately, my teachers couldn't tell me how to make nontoxic paints, and the books I found on the topic were outdated and difficult to understand. I began experimenting with making my own watercolors using berries and mud, which led me down a pathway to discovery of nontoxic color. Hands-on experience opened my eyes and helped me to develop a love for plant-based color. Eventually, that love of botanical color brought me to travel to organic farms and school gardens across America, and to delve into the textile history of many cultures around the world. I discovered that many of the answers to my questions lay in the long history of the handmade.

HISTORY and COLOR

Working with plant-based color is a craft that holds insight into natural science, and puts you in touch with the long history of inspired human design. Botanical pigments and dyes have been used for thousands of years for cultural expression and individual creativity. Natural dyeing is not unlike cooking and, in fact, many of the same principles apply.

Creating your own recipes, gathering the freshest materials, timing, and alchemy all play integral roles in both the culinary and dyeing arts. Natural dyes were most likely discovered through the process of cooking plants for food and for creating medicine.

We know that humans have used plant-based materials to dye their clothing and other items for thousands of years. Brilliant, lasting botanical colors have been found in ancient murals and in the clothing and objects at burial sites of ancient peoples. Spanish explorers found textile products in the Americas that had been colored with the red extract of the cochineal, a tiny beetle. That brilliant red dye, as well as other natural dyes like saffron and indigo, were extremely valuable trade commodities around the globe for centuries.

The first synthetic dye was invented in 1856, when an English chemist looking for the cure to malaria accidentally discovered a synthetic version of mauve. Textile producers found that synthetics were cheaper, easier to apply, and more colorfast, and they could be produced in a brighter range of colors. Natural dyes quickly fell from favor, replaced by synthetic dyes. Among the benefits and drawbacks industrial production brought was the increasing loss of knowledge of plant-based color.

But in the 1990s, environmental concerns aroused renewed interest in natural coloring, and several countries prohibited the use of chemical dyes. The future of natural dyeing is exciting, since we can learn from textile history and can innovate with modern technologies. The European Union is currently working to limit oil-based dye products and is creating initiatives to revive organic, sustainable, and renewable sources of plant-based dyes.

The loss of traditional dye knowledge is much the same as grocery store shopping when all you see are four different types of apples in the produce section rather than the hundreds of varieties of apples that actually exist. We have forgotten, in only a few generations, the vast majority of organic sources of color.

The silvery gray color on this hemp and silk fabric was created from a traditional Pomo Indian recipe using acorns, iron, and lemon.

CONNECTING WITH the SOURCE

One of my greatest motivations for creating this book on natural plant dyes came from experimenting with organic recipes for color. Books and information on natural dyeing are diverse, and dye-producing plants and dye recipes differ from region to region.

As I gathered my information, I realized that many natural dye recipes have been lost to particular cultures and regions because of large-scale industry. Biodiversity for dyes has suffered the same fate as food: cheap and environmentally damaging processes have wreaked havoc on both nature and culture.

Natural dyes have a rich history in every culture on the planet. Looking to our past for the stories of traditional dyes is a powerful way of uncovering interesting ideas and techniques. In textile history, there are countless examples of sustainable processes used by our ancestors around the globe, and you can also find many examples of practices that are unsustainable. Learning from our past and evolving sustainable techniques is crucial to preserving our planet. The natural world is intrinsically regenerative. The conversation must be reopened so that we learn from nature, and can participate in rather than interfere with natural processes.

In the past several decades, the Slow Food movement has taken hold internationally in reaction to fast food and the speed and thoughtlessness of modern life, and promotes organic, local, and carefully created food. Just as the Slow Food movement is growing, so are the fields of Slow Fashion and Slow Textiles. A tenet of the Slow Textiles movement is that clothing and textiles, as with food, often lose their connection to quality ingredients and health when mass-produced. So balance is key, and designing from a "slow" perspective is about true care and stewardship for both nature and culture. The idea of slowness doesn't refer to how long it takes to make or do something, but is about awareness, accountability, and responsibility for our everyday actions, and supporting a more fulfilling experience for individuals and communities through a process of full participation.

These blackberries were wild harvested and steeped in the sun in a glass jar for brilliant color. Using cold-water dye baths and letting the sun do the color extraction is an easy, energy-saving method.

An example of a Slow Textile dyeing project is a fabric that is dyed with ecologically low-impact methods from renewable non-toxic plant materials and repurposed natural, nontoxic fiber. All stages of the project, from the source of the fabric and the process of creating it to the ultimate purpose of the dyed fabric, are considered for sustainability. Exploring from a "slow" perspective can unlock practices for cleaner ways of creating our clothing and textiles with artistry, designing like nature does, with no waste and with incredible beauty.

Using regenerative design methods, or methods that contribute to nature rather than deplete it, allows us amazing opportunities to collaborate in sustainable ways with the plants in our gardens, neighborhoods, and communities. A simple example of a regenerative design practice is dyeing with onionskins, which create a nontoxic color from a natural plant by-product. The used dye matter can then become compost and nutrients for your plants, which you can use again for future dyeing projects.

As with food, natural fibers and dyes were once cultural examples of what was available in a bioregion. The natural dye plants you find growing in Maine, for example, are very different from those in California or in Hawaii. Getting to know your landscape, cultural history, and bioregion can bring inspiration to the creative process. Speaking with those who are local to a region will often help lead you to ideas and adventures with color. This can be a first step in building authentic, place-based creativity.

Food, clothing, and shelter—three basic plant-based human needs—have become more and more abstract in our daily lives. Like food and shelter, clothing is a necessity as well as a mode of personal and cultural expression. In my work as a textile artist, I became aware of just how connected sustainable fashion and textiles are to the organic food movement, since the majority of our clothing and textiles come from mass-produced sources, without fair trade, and create immense environmental pollution in the process.

{ CONTINUED } ·············➤

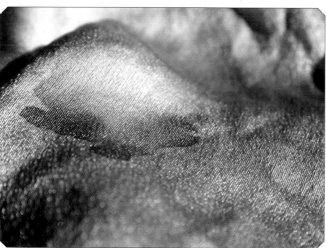

ABOVE: *Japanese maple leaves can create shades of pink to deep gray.* **BELOW:** *Crushing nasturtiums into fabric dyed with acorn and iron creates a bright spot of color.*

My interest in nontoxic and regenerative color sources brought me to work with the Edible Schoolyard, a nonprofit one-acre garden project in Berkeley, California, that teaches kids to grow their own organic food and make delicious meals, as part of the public school curriculum. In recognizing the general lack of knowledge about our material culture and where things come from, and the lack of cross-disciplinary dialogue among environmental movements, I became aware that education and experimentation are crucial in order to move forward in a truly sustainable, even regenerative way. I started the Permacouture Institute in 2007, a nonprofit organization that supports educational and research programs on dye and fiber plants and on social practices for sustainability in fashion and textiles. Working with a biodiversity of fibers and dyes and with organics is a very important step in seeking long-term sustainability in our clothing and textiles.

LEFT: *Botanical dye sources can yield luscious, soft colors.*
CENTER: *The bright colors of these farmers market poppies can inspire us to create a range of dye colors.*
RIGHT: *Poppy flowers just opening up hold brilliant as well as subtle colors to be admired.*

OPPOSITE PAGE, ABOVE: *Garden plants can be beautiful and functional. Calendula can be made into a healing salve as well as a colorful dye bath.* **OPPOSITE PAGE, BELOW:** *When viewed up close, a calendula flower on the edge of bloom can inspire textile design ideas.*

HOW TO USE THIS BOOK

There is often an assumption that natural dyeing is ecofriendly, green, and safe. But this is true only if the botanical dyeing is done in an informed, environmentally responsible way, and with plants that are grown organically and harvested and disposed of appropriately. This book offers you guidance on collecting botanical dye materials, growing dye plants yourself, and dyeing many fibers, materials, and projects in an easy, sustainable, and safe way.

Natural dye recipes and tips on collecting or growing botanical dye materials are the core of this book. I start the book by discussing dyeing basics, including the equipment you'll need, what to consider in setting up a workplace, what the dyeing process involves step by step, and the kinds of plant materials you'll want to collect for making dyes. Foraging for wild plant material can be especially inspiring, so I give you lots of ideas for plants and trees to look for throughout the seasons and I suggest what to know about gathering plant parts responsibly. I also talk about how to create a dye garden, whether it's a raised bed in your backyard or pots in your apartment, and I discuss many familiar plants you can easily cultivate for vibrant color.

Sprinkled throughout the book are discussions of which plants yield which dye colors, recipes for a broad range of colors, and guidance for numerous projects to make with natural dyes, all accompanied by photographs. So that you can quickly know the range of colors you can get from certain botanical dyes, I've included a color chart of hues and shades you can create from plant dyes provided in the book. I am dedicated to using sustainability principles in my work, so throughout the book I provide information on how you can use ecofriendly habits when going about the process of dyeing textiles. You may want to get involved in community sharing of dyeing traditions, and therefore I've provided a list of resources for finding dyeing materials, helpful hints on dyeing and gardening, and dyeing organizations.

I wrote this book to encourage exploration for biodiversity in materials and to cultivate a joy of creating color from the most surprising and simple plant-based sources. As you get started on your journey of making your own plant dyes, I hope you will be as continually awed by the process as I am.

Chapter 1

Nature often has ways of catching and storing water, like in this spider web.

Plant Dyeing Basics

Getting Started

Natural dyeing is much like cooking, which may be why I love the process. Cooking and dyeing share the process of using recipes, finding the right ingredients, experimentation, and timing. And the two arts use many of the same elements to do the work, from cooking pots to a heat source to chemistry. Much of color chemistry for the natural dye process also depends upon sourcing the right plant materials at the peak of their freshness. Natural dyes love natural fibers and porous natural materials. Once you've extracted the dye color from your plant material, you can dye almost anything that is made of a natural fibrous material—yarn, fabric, old clothes, new clothes, ribbon—practically anything you can think of.

Again, much like cooking, each ingredient, or plant source, will lend its own basic color extraction properties. As you explore the alchemy of color, your dye pot soon will be blooming with a wide range of hues.

Suri alpaca wools were dyed with fallen leaves from different trees in my urban neighborhood.

EQUIPMENT AND SAFETY

The utensils used for making plant-based color are often the same kinds of equipment you use in cooking food. But make sure that you have your own equipment for dyeing. You don't want to confuse your dyeing equipment with your kitchen utensils or pots used for food preparation. Some materials you will use in dyeing are not edible, so you'll need equipment that you use only for dyeing and that you keep in your dyeing workplace.

Second-hand stores and yard sales are great places to find equipment for dyeing. Dye pots should be large enough to immerse your fabric so it has enough room to dye evenly, and so you can stir the fabric easily without the pot overflowing. Having a lid for the dye pot is also helpful to make water heat faster and to keep smells and fumes from getting into the air. You'll want your dye pots to have secure lids, especially for when you soak fibers overnight or more, so you don't have children or animals tampering with your dyestuff.

For essential dyeing equipment, I recommend using stainless steel dyeing pots, because that metal will not affect or modify your dye color. Most of the equipment should be stainless steel or glass, which are easier to clean. Basic dyeing equipment you'll want to slowly collect could include:

- [ ] a food scale, which measures ounces and grams as well as pounds
- [ ] stainless steel pots of different sizes, with lids
- [ ] glass or stainless steel tubs or bowls of different sizes
- [ ] stainless steel strainers of different sizes, including a very fine strainer for scooping up bits of plant material in the dye bath
- [ ] glass measuring cups of various sizes
- [ ] stainless steel measuring spoons
- [ ] a mortar and pestle
- [ ] stir sticks, stainless steel utensils, or wood dowels; keep separate sticks for iron dye baths
- [ ] wood or plastic cutting boards for preparing plant materials
- [ ] cotton cheesecloth or silk fabric for straining fine-particle dye material
- [ ] stainless steel cooking scissors for cutting up plants
- [ ] glass jars for mordant solutions
- [ ] glass containers with tight lids for storing dyes or other dye materials
- [ ] plastic buckets for soaking, washing, and rinsing your fibers
- [ ] a cooking thermometer, with a range of 50°F to 200°F (10°C to 93°C)
- [ ] stainless steel tongs for stirring and retrieving your fibers from your dye solutions
- [ ] large glass jars and bowls for solar dyeing
- [ ] a heat source for indoor or outdoor dyeing
- [ ] labels and a permanent marking pen for identifying and labeling your materials once they are dried
- [ ] a sturdy drying rack or clothesline for hanging your fabrics to dry
- [ ] clothespins

Dyeing equipment is much like what you use for cooking. Good quality, large stainless steel pots are essential companions in the dyeing process.

As you do your own natural dyeing projects, you may discover other helpful equipment to add to this list, to make your creative experience more organized, safe, and pleasurable.

When you are working with natural dyes, many parts of your body may come in contact with the dye bath: hands, arms, legs, torso, face. Taking care of your skin as you work with botanical color is very important. Wearing gloves to protect your hands is essential. Even nontoxic organic materials can be irritants, and you can absorb them through your eyes, nose, and lungs, so when working with some materials you will want to wear a mask. If you are using hot-water dyes, you may want to wear a splash apron and rubber boots. Important safety equipment includes:

- ☐ **covered shoes, or heat-resistant boots**
- ☐ **waterproof, heat-resistant gloves**
- ☐ **old clothes you use only for dyeing**
- ☐ **a splash-proof smock or apron**
- ☐ **a dust mask**
- ☐ **a vapor mask**

{ CONTINUED } ·············▸

For dyeing, you need a few good pots to work with, reserved only for dyeing.

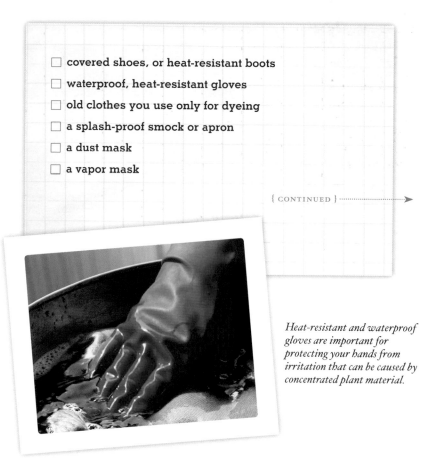

Heat-resistant and waterproof gloves are important for protecting your hands from irritation that can be caused by concentrated plant material.

LEFT: *Fennel can yield gorgeous shades of yellow and green on silk and wool textiles.*
CENTER: *This fennel dye bath is being stored for later use in a large glass jar.*
RIGHT: *The fruit of the fig tree is edible, but the milky white sap of the stems can be an irritant to your skin.*

The dye recipes in this book use nontoxic and even edible sources. But as you get involved in dyeing, it's crucial for you to build up your own store of knowledge about dye materials. Just because something is deemed natural does not necessarily mean that it is entirely safe to work with or healthy for you. Know what you are working with before it goes into the dye pot.

A good example of a dye plant that has a harmful by-product is the fig tree (*Ficus carica*). The fruit is edible and delicious, and you may want to use the fig leaves for dyeing, which provide a vibrant yellow to green, but the stems of fig leaves have a tree sap that is toxic and should be handled carefully. The leaves themselves are safe to use, so I cut the leaves from the stems with scissors and I avoid the stem sap, leaving it out of the dye bath. The sap of fig stems is a milky white, which is usually an indicator in nature that a sap is poisonous. Among the many leaves that should be carefully considered for their toxicity are those from peach and plum trees (*Prunus* species), which contain cyanide, and rhubarb leaves, which contain oxalic acid.

If you have come across a plant you want to experiment with or a dye recipe you want to try and are unsure of its toxicity, study up on it before dyeing with it. Many books and Web sites discuss the various characteristics of plants. It is important to look at both dye sources and botanical sources, since it is difficult to get complete and useful plant information from just one or the other field. Once you have taken steps to be knowledgeable in your work, creating color from botanical sources can be as easy as making your favorite tea.

SETTING UP A WORKPLACE

My dyeing studio is behind my house in my garden. If you live in a climate that allows working outdoors through the seasons, I'd recommend setting up your workspace outdoors. I love working outdoors when dyeing, because for me the outdoors is an endless source of creativity. Your senses are often more alive around the smells, colors, and tactile qualities of nature. And being outdoors gives you plenty of room. It is also an excellent way to be closer to sources of water, your garden of dye plants, and your compost pile for disposing of materials. There's plenty of natural airflow, and it also offers easy cleanup.

Having a big, stable worktable is crucial for dyeing. I have a large stainless steel kitchen table that can be moved around in my yard, for sun or shade. You will also need to have a safe place, like a shed you can close and lock, to store your dye materials away from the weather and from children and pets.

If you live in a small house or apartment without outdoor access, you can work in the kitchen and use the stove for heating dyes. Indoors, make sure you are working with nontoxic plant materials and mordants. If the plant is an edible one, you usually know you are safe. You will also need to make sure you have proper cross-ventilation in your workspace. If you have a vent above your stove, turn it on to suck out dye fumes. And while you're working, open some windows to allow air to circulate to ensure that vapors don't collect in your living space. Make sure that your cooking utensils and foodstuffs are covered with drop cloths to keep dust and vapors from collecting on them.

ABOVE: *Working outdoors is an ideal way to access your dye material, have plenty of ventilation, and allow your wet textiles to drip dry. My dye garden and studio are one and the same.*
BELOW: *A greenhouse is a good place to keep plants warm over the winter, get your dye plants started early, and can be a weatherproof and ventilated option for a year-round studio.*

NATURAL FIBERS and NATURAL DYES

Knowing about fibers and the differences among them is essential in choosing a fabric and dyeing it successfully. Knowing the difference between natural and synthetic fibers can be very valuable, as it will lead you to know how to repurpose old fabrics and yarns with a colorful new life.

The more I've learned about biodiversity and fibers, the more I have gotten excited about how many alternative natural fibers there are to work with. Natural fibers for dyeing come from a huge diversity of animals and plants. Traditional cultures created textiles from a broad range of fibers according to what was available or locally grown. Numerous animals produce fiber you can experiment with, from angora rabbits to cashmere goats, merino sheep, and suri alpacas. Purchasing wool supplies from local farmers at farmers markets or even raising your own fiber can be very satisfying ways of connecting with your materials and to the people who grew them while at the same time supporting local farms.

Finding natural fibers to dye can be easy if you're looking at garments that have tags telling composition of fabrics but can be tricky when you are searching for fabrics at scrap centers. A simple way to establish whether a fiber in a shop is natural or synthetic is to ask the shopkeeper to do a burn test, which involves taking a corner of the fabric and setting it aflame with a match. If the fabric melts and shrivels, it's made from synthetic materials, but if the fiber burns, it is a natural fiber.

Not surprisingly, natural dyes love natural fibers. The many kinds of wool are generally the most versatile, as natural dyes bond well to the fiber. Wool fiber will also attach to a wider variety of dyes than plant-based fibers, such as cotton. Organic sheep wool, for instance, can be an ecologically smart choice. Sheep thrive on weeds and are often used to replace both lawnmowers and unhealthy pesticides in farms and gardens. Organic wool is not only biodegradable but can also be excellent garden mulch.

Depending on the dye you use, plant-based fibers can take longer to prepare. Plant-based fibers more often require a mordant; applying a premordant of tannin and then alum can often produce more lightfast and vibrant color.

OPPOSITE PAGE, ABOVE: *Raw silk spun on a cone can be dyed in skeins for weaving, knitting, or other textile projects.*
OPPOSITE PAGE, BELOW: *Peace silk and organic wool fabrics can be good choices for dyeing. Yardage can be hand-dyed at home. Just make sure you have a dye pot large enough for the fabric to move freely in the water and take the dye evenly.*

Wool needs to be treated gently in the dye bath. Heat the water gradually, to avoid agitating the fibers and causing them to mat and felt.

In natural dyeing, it's important to use a biodiversity of fibers and dyes because different plants and animals take different resources out of the ecosystem, as well as giving back different vital resources. As monocropping has shown, growing one crop in the same place repeatedly will deplete the soil, and the risk of pests and diseases will also greatly increase.

Producing and consuming organic fibers is also important. Not only is it healthier for the land, water, and air to grow livestock and plants organically, but it is also important for the wearer of the garment or textile, in relation to off-gassing issues of toxic chemicals, and it is important for textile waste and disposal. Organic fibers and dyes will biodegrade without releasing further toxic by-products into the ecosystem. Currently, many of the crops that produce the fibers used to make our clothing and home wares—often those we sleep in every night—account for some of the highest pesticide usage across all agricultural practices. It takes roughly one-third of a pound of chemicals (pesticides and fertilizers) to grow enough cotton for just a single T-shirt, which is why it is especially important to consider organic cotton and other fibers for even the most basic of textile goods. On the flip side, you can have an organic fiber T-shirt, but perhaps the dyes used to color it were toxic. And toxic dyes will also prevent the organic T-shirt from being biodegradable.

Growing organic fibers and dyes uses agricultural methods designed to help sustain the land they grow on, the people who grow and harvest them, and the planet in general. Even though we do not literally eat or drink our clothing, our food and water are dependent on the same soil, air, and water. Our food crops and textile crops are often grown in the same bioregions. In terms of the importance of organic livestock for fibers, organic fibers and the animals that produce them are not dipped in insecticides to control external parasites. And organic livestock farmers are required to ensure that they do not overstep the natural capacity of the land on which the animals graze. These are important contributions to the health and well-being of environmental systems. Fiber, like any sustainable material, should be traced back to its origin to make sure the animal is being humanely raised and processed. Look for organic and fair-trade labeling when buying new fibers. When you get fiber that is from an animal that was raised organically, you know that the fiber is better for the environment and for your skin.

Animal Fibers

Animal-based, or protein, fibers are naturally biodegradable. Examples are sheep wool, alpaca hair, angora, cashmere, and silk, which come in a variety of colors, from cream to shades of gray, brown, and black. These fibers are obtained by shearing or combing the hair from the animal, so they are entirely sustainable. Protein fibers often absorb natural dyes very well without additional treatments, which makes them easier for beginning dyers to work with. The numerous animal fibers you can use for your dyeing projects include:

ALPACA. The alpaca is a domesticated South American camelid, which resembles a small llama. Alpaca is a super soft, luxurious fiber that is also warm, light, and durable. It accepts dyes well, making it a favorite of many hand-dyers. A great benefit of using alpaca fiber for your project is that many small farms in America subsidize their crops by raising alpacas and selling the wool, so you can often find alpaca wool in local farmers markets with a low related carbon footprint: because it is raised domestically or even locally, it requires less travel and therefore fuel and energy consumption. Alpaca fiber does not contain lanolin and therefore requires less preparation for dyeing. Alpaca fiber is supple and can be turned into yarns for a wide variety of items like weavings, knits, rugs, and other textile items. If you are buying alpaca from another country, research the source, since alpaca wool and especially baby alpaca fiber can often come with fair-trade and political issues attached.

ANGORA. Angora fiber comes from the angora rabbit. The fiber is very silky and soft, and is a favorite for knitting projects, as well as weavings and other handmade items. Angora fiber is easy to dye and can be blended well with other fibers. You can even raise your own angora rabbits for fiber; they will not only eat much of your kitchen food waste, but can create compost for your garden as well.

CASHMERE. Cashmere is an extremely soft, fine fiber that comes from the belly of the cashmere goat. Cashmere goats are rare—they live in the high-altitude regions of central Asia—so the fiber is expensive. Cashmere fiber is notable for providing extremely lightweight but good insulation. The fibers are easy to spin, and the yarn can be made into light but very warm clothing.

SILK. The most common type of silk comes from the cocoon of the mulberry silkworm in captivity. But many other types of silks exist and can come from other types of insect larvae. When purchasing new silk for dyeing, you may want to consider buying peace silk, or raw tussah silk. Wild silks are not factory farmed but are collected naturally. Peace silk is a more sustainable, humane option than most other silks, in which the larva is sacrificed when harvesting the cocoon. In peace silk, the silkworms are allowed to emerge as moths before the cocoon is used as fiber. Peace silk production is less toxic and less polluting, since bleaching and degumming processes are restrained. There are many types of peace silk available as more ecofriendly dyeing material.

SHEEP WOOL. Wool absorbs most natural dyes well, making it an ideal fiber to work with. Wool fiber can vary in strength, color, texture, and weight, depending on the animal and the part of the animal it comes from. Sheep wool is a favored fiber to dye, because it will bind to a wider variety of natural dyes than plant-based fibers such as cotton, and often is the easiest and most successful fiber to work with if you choose to forego a mordant.

Plant Fibers

Plant-based, or cellulose, fibers are also naturally biodegradable. Again, it is important to support organic plant-based fibers, since as agricultural products they are better for land stewardship, plants, and people. Some of the more widely used plant fibers for dyeing include:

COTTON. Cotton is a plant native to tropical and subtropical regions around the world, including the Americas, India, and Africa. Cotton is the most widely used natural cloth fiber on the market today. Cotton fiber most often is spun into yarn or thread that is woven into a soft, breathable textile or fabric.

BAMBOO. Bamboo fabric is a natural textile made from the pulp of the bamboo plant. Bamboo fabric is light and strong, has excellent wicking properties (it absorbs water and sweat away from the skin to the edges of the fabric), and is somewhat antibacterial, which makes it ideal for activewear. Bamboo is relatively new as a fiber for fashion and textiles and is produced using the same technology as for viscose fibers. Bamboo fiber has a silky smooth sheen and efficiently absorbs and retains dyes. Bamboo is marketed as an ecofriendly fiber, but these claims should be carefully considered. Although bamboo as a plant is a renewable resource, the process by which bamboo is currently processed is energy and chemical intensive.

HEMP. Hemp is an amazing fiber. The hemp plant grows quickly, and does not need pesticides because it does not attract pests. Hemp fibers are processed from the stalk of the plant, and are longer, stronger, and more absorbent than cotton. Fabrics made of at least 50 percent hemp block out the sun's rays more effectively than other fibers. Hemp fiber can used for many types of fabric, as well as for paper, twine, and thread.

LINEN. A textile made from the fibers of the flax plant is called linen. Linen textiles are some of the oldest textiles in the world, going back many thousands of years. Linen is valued for its exceptional coolness in hot weather. Linen is spun from the long fibers found just behind the bark in the multilayer flax stem. This cellulose fiber from the stem can be spun and is used in the production of linen thread, cordage, and twine. Household items made from linen become more supple and soft to the touch with use. That's why linen has long been a traditionally preferred bedding material.

Preparing Animal Fibers for Dyeing

Before you work with fibers or fabrics for dyeing, you must first scour your material, or wash until clean. Scouring ensures that the fabrics are free from natural oils, dirt, or grime, or any residue from chemical processing, starching, or bleaching. For example, wool right off the sheep, or raw wool, often contains lanolin, a natural protective oil, and if the wool is not scoured, the lanolin can keep the dye from bonding on the fiber. Scouring is an important step in dyeing, since any dirt or residue can prevent color from adhering evenly to the fibers: the dye cannot seep fully into the fiber and will wash off, leaving an unsuccessful result.

I scour natural fibers in a big bowl of cool or lukewarm water, using 2 teaspoons of ecofriendly, gentle, pH-neutral dishwashing liquid soap, which you can get at your local grocery store, instead of the traditional scouring agent that many dye books recommend. Then I rinse the fiber several times in cool or warm water until the water runs clear of any dirt or soap residue. After scouring and rinsing, soak your fiber for at least an hour or overnight in clear water before dyeing it. This step helps the fiber to accept full and even mordanting and dyeing. Fibers and fabric can be gently wrung and then placed directly into the dye or mordant bath after soaking.

{ CONTINUED } ·······················➤

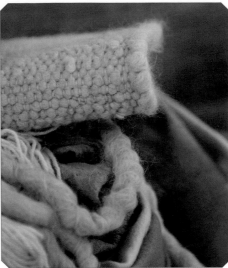

LEFT: *Let your fibers and fabrics soak in water before dyeing for at least an hour and preferably overnight, to encourage the fiber to accept the dye molecules.*
RIGHT: *All kinds of fiber can be dyed, from raw materials to vintage clothing and readymade rugs.*

OPPOSITE PAGE, LEFT: *Dyeing small swatches as tests of your dye bath helps you know what color and effect you may get before working with larger projects. Keep the swatches in a dyer's recipe and swatch book for future reference.*
OPPOSITE PAGE, RIGHT: *Keeping dye swatches on cards can be handy reminders of your dyes' lightfastness and washfastness.*

Animal fibers like wool do not like sudden changes in water temperature: they will shrink or mat with hot water or rapid changes from hot to cold water and vice versa. Silk should be processed at even slightly lower temperatures than wool so it does not lose its luster. All natural fibers should be treated gently and not rubbed against each other, which will cause friction and matting of the fiber.

Silk has a natural protective gum layer that binds two fibrous filaments of a silk fiber. Silk gum is typically left on the raw silk until it is ready to dye, and silk must be degummed before you dye it. Removing the gum from the fiber improves the sheen, color, hand, and texture of the silk. Many commercial silk yarns are sold fully degummed, but it is advisable to degum your silk yarn just to make sure before dyeing.

Preparing Plant Fibers for Dyeing

To thoroughly clean cellulose, or vegetable, fibers such as cotton and linen, simmer for at least 2 hours in a pH-neutral liquid soap and washing soda solution. You can find washing soda, or sodium carbonate, in the laundry section of most supermarkets as well as from on-line retailers. It can be caustic, so wear gloves when working with it. Or you can soak the fabric in the soap-soda solution in a large glass jar for 2 days, as for sun tea, allowing the heat from the sun and the steeping time to achieve the cleansing process.

To clean vegetable fibers, to a pot of water I add 2 teaspoons of liquid soap, and I use 1 tablespoon of washing soda for each gallon of soapy water. Cotton contains lots of built-up waxes and oils, so a longer, more rigorous treatment should be used to remove the oils and other debris from the fabric. Store-bought cottons and similar fabrics can contain industry bleaches or starches that can prevent natural dyes from binding, so thorough scouring and soaking is often necessary before mordanting and dyeing. Linen contains less wax and fewer filaments, so it does not need to be cleaned as vigorously. Fibers do not need to be dried before dyeing and can go directly from being soaked to the dye pot.

KEEPING A RECIPE AND SWATCH BOOK

Keeping a recipe and swatch book can be a very helpful part of learning the natural dye process. Natural dyes are not as widely documented as commercial synthetic dye processes. Natural dyeing also depends on numerous varying factors for successful results, including length of time in the dyeing process, amount of heat, freshness of plant material used, parts of the plant used, type of water, method of dyeing, type of mordant, and just general alchemy. When you get a successful result, it is best to record the process, much like writing down the recipe for a new dish you want to make again. Recording your dye recipes is a good way to ensure that you can repeat those colors you love. Keeping little swatches, or fabric samples, from the dye recipes allows you to have a piece of the actual color you created so you can try to match it in the future.

Creating a recipe and swatch book can be as easy as saving bits of yarn or fabric every time you dye, and pinning them to a sample card. On the back of the card, you can write down your recipe, include the date of your experiment, and any other notes about the method you used. You can also use plastic sleeves in a three-ring binder, so you can flip through to recipes and results when you are dyeing and not worry about the samples getting wet.

Keeping swatches also allows you to test a dye for color fastness when washed, exposed to light, and other fugitive color qualities of the plants you are working with. For instance, you can test to see whether your fabric is lightfast by leaving a piece of the cloth in the sun, and covering half with a solid heavy object, then checking the fabric after a day or two to see what sun exposure has done to the dye on the exposed portion. Then save the swatch in your book with your notes about it.

Once you get in the habit of keeping a recipe and swatch book, you'll find that it's just like having a sketchbook or journal. It's a great place to keep all your color experiments and results, and you'll be able to use it to get inspired.

Drawing can also be an integral part of keeping dyeing records and learning more about the plants and materials you work with. Drawings can be especially helpful for identifying dye-producing plants, and for learning more about the qualities of the plant. When you draw a plant, you sit with that plant and truly focus on its unique characteristics. You copy the features of that plant and get to know all its tiny details, allowing you to know the plant more intimately and to be able to spot the plant quickly in the future.

THE IMPORTANCE OF WATER

Dyeing is dependent upon water, lots of water, at many steps in the process. Being an environmentally aware natural plant dyer includes being knowledgeable not only about the source of your dye materials but also about how you obtain and use water.

If you are working with tap water from the grid, you'll want to be mindful of not wasting it. Use just enough water for your project. You can also conserve water by using your dye baths for multiple projects, so you get as much use out of the color as possible. Also use biodegradable, nontoxic soaps, so the used dye water can be poured down the sink or among your garden plants without causing environmental damage.

You'll need to know the pH level of the water from your tap, because whether your tap water is acid or alkaline can play a role in how color is created in the dye pot. Tap water varies from one community and region to another. To achieve consistent results with your dyeing, test your water's pH level with a simple pH strip available at the hardware store. A pH of 7 is considered neutral on a scale of 1 to 14. A pH of 1 is very acidic, while anything above 7 is considered alkaline and 14 is the most alkaline. Neutral water (pH 7) is considered the best water for dyeing, to get consistency of color results. Neutral water should also be used for washing and rinsing your fiber before and after dyeing. If your water is too acidic, you can make it more neutral with washing soda, ground chalk, or wood ash. If your water is too alkaline, you can neutralize it with clear vinegar or lemon juice.

Some dye plants are pH indicators, allowing us to tell whether the water being used from the tap is on the more acid side or the alkaline side. With red cabbage dye, for instance, by the color of the dye you achieve in the water, you can see that the water in San Francisco is much more acidic than the water in Copenhagen. The dye color acts like a litmus test—whether it tends more toward purple or blue—with purple being more acidic and blue being more alkaline.

Many dyers, however, are happy with a less regimented approach to natural dyeing. They enjoy the surprise of what colors develop in the dye pot, without testing the water pH first. That's a fun way to work, too.

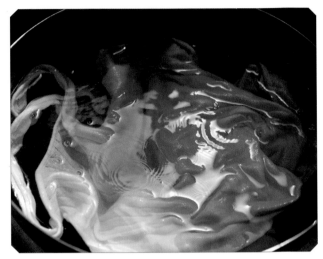

It's important to know what is in the water from your tap, so that you can get accurate color results. A pH strip can be purchased at the hardware store for analyzing your tap water.

Red cabbage is a natural pH indicator. You can usually tell how acidic or alkaline your water is by how purple or blue your dye color is.

LEFT: *Planting on a warm spring afternoon. Just as with cooking, gardening is a good way to get in sync with the rhythms of nature.* **CENTER:** *Water in the garden.* **RIGHT:** *Rainwater is excellent for natural dyeing because it is soft water, which allows brighter colors to emerge in the dye bath.*

Collecting Rainwater

Rain can be used as a resource. Collecting rainwater is a sustainable way to use nonpotable water and not overuse a precious resource. Rainwater is an excellent water supply for dyeing, because it is soft water: it contains few minerals, making it ideal for achieving vibrant, clear color. Tap water is often hard, containing a high content of minerals like magnesium and calcium. In dyeing, the minerals can combine with the washing soda, creating soap scum, which could, in the case of exceptionally hard water, cause problems such as spotting in your dyed fabric. To make your hard water softer, you can use water softeners in your tap water, or you can use distilled or spring water as your dye water.

Catching and using rainwater is a significant way to integrate a sustainable practice into the craft of natural dyeing. If you live in a place where you could collect rainwater, harvesting it can be as easy as collecting water from your rooftop in an old barrel under your downspout and storing the water in a storage tank. The stored rainwater can be used for your dyeing projects as well as for watering the plants in your garden. Using rainwater is an ideal way to minimize grid water usage.

A rainwater barrel for collecting water can be anything, like an old industrial food container. Ask restaurants or co-ops in your area whether they have a barrel they no longer need. Make sure your rain barrel is positioned to collect water by the time the fall rains are scheduled to occur in your area. Over the fall, winter, and spring, you should be able to collect enough water to use in the dry season. Your rainwater barrel should have a sturdy, fitted lid, so that the water is secure from children, animals, and insects, especially mosquitoes that might lay their eggs in it.

Using Saltwater

Saltwater can be used in natural dyeing. It is a renewable natural resource, and if you are fortunate enough to live near the ocean or a bay, it may be easy for you to collect. The alkalinity of saltwater can offer interesting results for many dye experiments. And saltwater can also be a modifier or additive for dye recipes that require alkalinity.

EXTRACTING NATURAL DYE COLOR
with COLD AND HOT WATER

Remember that extracting dye colors can be as easy as brewing tea. In the extraction process, you place the plant material in a stainless steel container with enough water to cover the fiber you wish to dye: 1 gallon (4 l) of water for every 4 ounces (113 g) of fiber should be enough water to cover the fiber and give it plenty of room so it takes the mordant evenly. Then you process the plant material with either cold or heat, to bring out the dye. Whether you decide to use cold or hot water extraction is based on the plant material you're working with. Some plants work well in cold water, but most plants respond best, just like tea, with a hot water process, to achieve the desired depth of color.

Some botanical dyes don't need heat to yield color, and can be processed successfully in cold water in 1 or 2 days to create dye. Some plant materials need a long soaking to yield color. Kinds of bark, for example, can take 1 to 2 weeks before enough dye will be extracted for colorful results.

To process plant material with hot water, bring the pot of water and plant material to a boil, turn down the heat to a simmer, 180°F (82°C), and simmer until the dye bath reaches the desired depth of color, usually within 20 minutes to 1 hour for most plants.

You can also extract color with heat through the solar method (see Solar Dyeing later in this chapter). This method saves energy since you are using the heat of the sun, and it is quicker than cold-water processing for most plants.

Regardless of the extraction method you use, when moving the fiber from one solution to another, make sure the dye bath or water temperature is similar to avoid shocking the fiber: move fiber from a simmering dye bath to a hot-water rinse, not cold, and move fiber from a cold-water dye bath to a cold-water rinse, not hot. Then gradually move the fiber to solutions from warm to cool, or cool to warm water temperatures.

Plant color can also be extracted onto your textile through direct application. Direct application can be as simple as pressing your dye plant into the cloth or beating the plant material into the cloth using a hammer or a rock.

OPPOSITE PAGE, ABOVE: *Cold-water dyeing can be used with some plants. Turmeric root can create a brilliant yellow.* **OPPOSITE PAGE, BELOW:** *Mix powdered turmeric root thoroughly in water to dissolve the pigment so you will get even absorption of color in your textile.*

COLD-WATER DYEING

Cold-water dyeing can be gentler on plant-based fibers, and requires little to no energy expenditure in the process. Many plants can be processed for dye with very little heat. Cold-water dyeing can be more successful when the concentration of plant material in the water is strong. If your recipe calls for heat extraction, to use cold water you will need to use more plant dye material in proportion to water for the extraction process.

It is important to remember that some plant dyes may not summon their true color without heat. In addition, some dyes may yield different colors with hot water than with cold-water dye processes. Madder root is a good example: with little or no heat, madder creates reds, and with overheating you get browns.

Cold-Water Dyeing of Animal Fibers

When working with animal fibers, first soak the fiber for at least 1 hour or even overnight to prepare it for color absorption. Then place the fiber in the cold dye bath, making sure it is submerged and there is plenty of room for it to dye evenly. You can use an old plate to weight the fiber and keep it submerged. Let the fiber soak overnight to see how much color is absorbed. For darker color, you can let the fiber soak up to several days. Check in on the fiber and gently stir occasionally. When the fiber is dyed the color you desire, wash it in cool water with a gentle pH-neutral soap, rinse thoroughly, and hang to dry.

Cold-Water Dyeing of Plant Fibers

Plant fiber can dye really well at room temperature. For best color results, soak vegetable fiber in the cold dye bath for several days or longer. To check for color results, wash the fiber with a pH-neutral soap, and rinse well. If the fiber still looks like it could be darker, return it to the dye bath and let it soak again for several more days. Then wash again, rinse thoroughly, and hang to dry.

HOT-WATER DYEING

When you begin to experiment with hot-water dyeing, it's important to remember to place the wet material you are dyeing into the warm liquid gradually so as not to shock or shrink the fiber, and then slowly raise the heat under the dye pot to the simmering point, 180°F (82°C). You can check the water temperature with a cooking thermometer. But as with cooking, you don't always need a thermometer, because you can gauge a dye pot's readiness to simmer by watching for the first signs of bubbles and then quickly reduce the heat to a low simmer. It's important to keep the dye bath below a boil in order to avoid losing the luster in silk fibers, or felting or shrinking wool materials. Simmer your fiber in the dye bath for 20 to 30 minutes, or until the fiber has taken on the color you desire. Gently stir the fiber so that it absorbs color evenly. If dyeing wool skeins, stir them gently in the water so as not to mat the fibers.

When color reaches the desired shade in the hot dye bath, lift the fiber out of the water, and wearing heat-resistant rubber gloves, gently squeeze the excess dye back into the dye pot. Then wash the fiber gently in warm to cool water with a gentle pH-neutral soap, and rinse thoroughly in cool water. Hang to dry.

If the dye is not exhausted (all dye has not been absorbed into the fiber), you can use the leftover dye bath to overdye, or redye, fabrics that have paled or to start another dye bath. And leftover dye can be saved for later use: pour into jars with tight lids, label contents, and store in a dark place.

SOLAR DYEING

Solar dyeing is a fun and easy way of experimenting with alternative energy sources for dyeing needs—in this case, using the sun's natural energy to heat your dye bath and bring color out of your plants.

The sun is a totally renewable energy source. Besides water, it is also important to consider where your energy or heat is coming from if you are using hot-water methods of dyeing your projects. Solar dyeing is another way of truly connecting to the source in every step of the process.

Solar dyeing with plants can be as easy as creating sun tea; in fact, it is nearly one and the same. Creating a solar dye system can be as simple as leaving your dye material in a big bowl of water in a warm, sunny spot out of reach from kids and pets. In the summer months, solar dyeing is often the way to go, since you can easily capture the hot summer rays. Whether you are a craft dyer or working to support greener ways of producing textiles, a solar heating system is a good example of smart production.

For the sun dyeing process, solar ovens can be made with readily available recycled materials, cheaply and quickly. You'll need two large cardboard boxes, one large enough to hold the other one with a 2- to 3-inch (5- to 8-cm) space between the walls. The smaller box should be large enough to hold your dye pot. Dark colored dye pots, rather than bright and shiny pots, are best when using a solar oven, because a dark pot will absorb the sun's heat quickly. To fully absorb the heat and to keep the solar energy trapped efficiently, pots must also have lids. Having a plexiglass lid cut to fit at a hardware store will give you a permanent cover for the solar oven and easy access to the interior of the oven. The materials you need and the building instructions and dyeing process are:

2 recycled cardboard boxes, which nest

Newspaper, several sheets, crumpled

Aluminum foil

Clear nontoxic tape

Black construction paper, several sheets

Large piece of cardboard, at least 2 inches (5 cm) bigger around than the top or the large box

Box cutter

Dye pot, containing dye bath and fiber

Plexiglass sheet cut to sit on top of the large box, or plastic wrap, or a clear, thick plastic bag

2 pot holders

To build the solar oven, line the bottom of the large box with the crumpled newspaper.

Place the small box inside the large box. Fill the space between the sides of the two boxes with crumpled newspaper.

Line the entire interior of the small box with aluminum foil, including the box flaps. Use the nontoxic tape to hold the foil in place, or fold the foil over the edges of the box flaps. Line the bottom of the small box with the black construction paper, to absorb heat.

{ CONTINUED } ·······················➔

Attaching foil to the interior surfaces of the small box.

To make the sun reflector, lay the piece of cardboard on top of the large box, and trace the shape of the box onto the cardboard. Add 2 inches (5 cm) around the trace line, then cut the cardboard with the box cutter, and cover the underside of the cardboard piece with aluminum foil. Smooth out any wrinkles in the foil, and secure the aluminum foil to the cardboard with the tape.

Attach the sun reflector to the back of the box with tape, to form a hinged lid, with the foiled side down.

Place the oven in the garden with the box lid up and the reflector facing the direction of the sun for maximum heat.

To dye fiber with the solar dyeing process, place your liquid dye materials and fiber into your dye pot, and place the dye pot inside the small box within solar oven. Close the flaps of the small box.

With the reflector lid up, cover the top of the large box with the plexiglass sheet, or the plastic wrap or the plastic bag, and secure around the top edge of the box with clear tape.

To create heat within the solar oven, the sun reflector should be up and facing the sun, to reflect the sun's rays down through the plastic top and into the oven.

After 3 or 4 hours, look in to check on how the dye bath is coming along. When you are satisfied with the color, carefully lift the plastic lid off the solar oven, and remove the dye pot, using pot holders since the lid and pot will be very hot.

A solar dyeing oven is fun to build and use, and making use of the sun's heat is an energy-efficient way to dye.

USING MORDANTS

A mordant is a fixative that allows dye molecules to bind to fiber. From the Latin word *mordere*, meaning to bite, a mordant is a chemical compound that can brighten a dye color, darken it, or make it colorfast. Using a mordant in the correct quantity and with the appropriate fiber can coax out a plant dye's full color spectrum and can extend lightfastness.

WHEN DO I NEED TO USE A MORDANT?

A mordant can be helpful and necessary depending on the dye and fiber combination you choose. Generally, animal fibers such as silk and wool are easier for the beginning dyer to experiment with as they are able to bond more readily with most plant dyes and take less time to mordant properly. Plant-based fibers, such as cotton, linen, and hemp, often benefit from premordanting with tannin and alum to achieve successful results. Some dyes in this book, such as Japanese maple and sour grass, were chosen for their easy compatibility with plant-based fibers even without a separate mordant, as the plant dye itself already contains tannins or other natural binders which act as built-in mordants. Please pay special attention to the recommended combinations of dye, mordant (or not), and fiber as you try the recipes and projects in this book.

Not all plant dyes need mordants to achieve good color. Some plants dyes already contain qualities that will bind color to fiber without any additives. Not using a mordant allows you more direct contact with the natural dye colors, which can be a simple, fascinating process, and can eliminate an extra step in the dyeing process, saving time, water, and energy. The key to successful results when you skip the use of a mordant relates to the plant materials you choose to make dye from, the fiber you want to dye, and the length of time it takes for the dye to set on the fiber.

My work with natural dyes at the Edible Schoolyard led me to explore plant dyes that could work without mordants, since they are as true to their original sources as possible and do not have additives potentially harmful to children. There are many nontoxic fruits, vegetables, roots, barks, and berries that contain dye compounds that, with the right fiber, will adhere directly to the fiber without mordanting, and these are the ones I use when working with young students.

Traditionally, many mordants have been solutions of dissolved metal oxides. But mordants from plant sources such as oak galls or acorns can work just as well on fibers. Choosing your mordant wisely is one way that you can create a more sustainable dyeing practice. In the 1970s, when many of my textile and natural dye mentors were working with natural color, metal mordants were used without proper protection. Many metal mordants, such as copper, tin, and chrome, are suggested in old natural dye books, as well as in recent ones. We now know that these metal mordants are toxic and should be avoided for the dyer's health as well as for the health of others. Many dyers now work only with alum and iron as metal mordants, since those are considered the safest to work with when used correctly.

Mordants can be used at different stages in the dyeing process: before dyeing as a premordant, as a mordant combined with the botanical dye, or after the fiber has been dyed as an aftermordant or modifier. When you use a premordant, you treat your undyed fiber or textile in a mordant bath before you dye it, which will then make the color bloom. You can store your premordanted fiber indefinitely for dyeing at a later stage (be sure to label the fiber), or you can dye it right away. Premordanting the fiber also assures that the mordant has properly bonded to the fiber before it goes into the plant dye bath, enhancing its effectiveness. You use the same mordant recipe whether the mordant is serving as a premordant, mordant, or aftermordant. Rinse mordanted fibers thoroughly, to eliminate loose mordant particles still clinging to the fiber.

Metal Mordants

Handle all mordants with care. When working with mordants, always wear gloves and a dust mask. And when working with mordants and heat, keep the mordants and dyes well below the boiling point so fumes aren't created that you might inhale.

The only metallic mordants we will be working with in this book are alum and iron. These mordants are nontoxic when used in the proper proportions. But they can be irritants and caustic, so work with them carefully to avoid any health hazards. When handled properly, alum and iron are excellent, easy mordants to use, to get long-lasting and even dramatic colors.

USING ALUM AS A MORDANT

Alum, or aluminum sulfate, is a substance found in the earth, and has been used as a mordant for thousands of years. Alum will brighten colors and will make many natural plant dyes colorfast. Since some plants love alum, you can often find it at gardening stores in the fertilizer section. And since it is used for pickling, you can usually get it at the grocery store in the spice section. Or try a specialty textile supplier. Alum can help extend the range of colors your plant dye can achieve, often allowing your dye pot to bloom into brighter and more intense color.

{ RECIPE }

BASIC ALUM MORDANT WITH WOOL

You can prepare alum mordant for hot dyeing, cold dyeing, or solar dyeing. This recipe gives instructions for the hot-dyeing method. Weigh the fiber you are going to dye when it is dry, and then measure the alum in proportion to the fiber's dry weight. Weigh the alum on a scale to get the proper amount. Before dyeing a natural fiber, soak it in water for at least a half-hour before putting it in the dye bath.

When using wool fiber, make sure the water temperature gradually rises or lowers, so the fiber can get used to the change. For most items, hang to dry. For delicate items like knitted wool sweaters and garments, it's best to lay them flat to dry so they keep their shape and don't stretch.

4 ounces (113 g) wool fiber

8 percent (1 1/2 teaspoons) alum to weight of fiber

7 percent (1 1/2 teaspoons) cream of tartar to weight of fiber

Soak the wool fiber in a bowl of water for at least 1 hour.

Place the alum and cream of tartar in a cup, add some boiling water, and stir to dissolve. Add the alum and cream of tartar mixture to a dye pot full of enough water to cover your fiber, and stir.

To the dye pot, add the previously soaked fiber you wish to mordant.

Place your dye pot on a burner. Bring the mordant solution to a simmer, 180°F (82°C), and simmer for 1 hour. Turn off the heat under the dye pot, and remove the fiber from the dye pot or allow the fibers to steep overnight.

Wash the fiber in water the same temperature as the dye bath with pH-neutral soap to remove unfixed mordant. Rinse the fiber thoroughly until the water runs clear, and hang to dry.

The spent alum bath can be disposed of down the drain (unless it is flows to a septic tank), along with plenty of running water. You can also pour the alum bath around your acid-loving plants.

Alum powder, seen here mixed with saffron, is an effective nontoxic metal mordant.

{ RECIPE }

BASIC ALUM MORDANT WITH SILK

You can process silk fabric with a mordant the same way you do wool and other natural fabrics. Weigh your silk fiber before measuring the alum; alum is used in proportion to the dry weight of the fiber. For silk, you can use either a cold-water or a hot-water dye method. This recipe is for the cold-water dye method.

4 ounces (113 g) silk fabric

8 percent (1 1/2 teaspoons) alum to weight of fiber

7 percent (1 1/2 teaspoons) cream of tartar to weight of fiber

Soak your silk fiber in water for at least 1 hour.

Put the alum and the cream of tartar in a cup, add some hot water, and stir to dissolve. Add the mordant mixture to a bucket of lukewarm water, and stir.

Put the wetted silk fabric into the mordant bath, and gently move it around in the bath for a few minutes. Leave the fabric to soak overnight.

Wash the fabric in cool water with pH-neutral soap to remove any unfixed mordant. Rinse thoroughly in cool water. Hang to dry.

USING IRON AS A MORDANT

When iron (ferrous sulfate) is used as a mordant, it often turns dye colors darker in tone. Iron is an earth-based substance, and we use it in powder form as a mordant material. It can be ordered from dye specialty stores or made yourself; a little goes a long way. Iron can be used as a premordant, but works just as well as an aftermordant. Iron can extend or alter the color from the initial dye bath. Iron usually takes effect very quickly, darkening the color or sometimes changing it completely.

Iron is a natural color modifier. Modifiers are usually applied to the dye bath to alter the color after the initial dyeing has occurred. Some modifiers, like iron, can also be mordants, but most modifiers change the color but do not help bind the color to the fiber unless a mordant has been used first. You can create iron liquid solution ahead of time and store it in clearly labeled in glass jars. One of the first traditional mordants was probably mud with a high level of iron in it. Ancient peoples may have become aware of iron's mordant abilities when watching leaves fall into iron-rich water and turn black from the chemical change.

Iron mordants should be labeled and safely stored. Iron is generally nontoxic in small doses, but can be potentially harmful and even fatal if swallowed in large quantities, especially by children and pets. Small amounts of iron are all you will ever use with fabric, since certain fibers, like wool and silk, have been known to fall apart over time if they have been treated with too much of this mordant.

It is important to always clean your pots well after mordanting fibers with iron. Iron mordant can leave a residue that can affect later dye baths by creating a duller or modified color, and can create unwanted spots on your fibers or textiles. Even a little bit of iron can cause colors to be more dull or gray versions of a dye color. You will want to keep a dye pot just for iron mordanting.

{ RECIPE }

BASIC IRON MORDANT WITH ANIMAL FIBER

Before dyeing your animal fiber, weigh the dry fiber and record the dry weight; the iron powder will be measured in proportion to the dry fiber weight. Iron powder can be obtained as ferrous sulfate crystals. You can mordant your fiber by heat, cold, or solar dyeing methods. When you're working with iron powder, be careful not to breathe in the iron dust, which can be caustic to the lungs. It's a good idea to wear a dust mask with iron powder.

4 ounces (113 g) fiber
2 percent (1/2 teaspoon) iron powder to weight of fiber

Wet the fiber in lukewarm water for at least 1 hour, or overnight.

Fill a large stainless steel pot with enough water to cover the fiber and give it plenty of room so it takes the mordant evenly.

Heat the water to a simmer, 180°F (82°C).

Put the iron powder in a cup, add some hot water, and stir to dissolve. Add the dissolved iron solution to the simmering water, and stir. Turn off the heat and let the water cool down.

Remove the soaking fiber from the water, and add it to the dye pot. Heat the mordant bath to a simmer. Put a lid on the pot to keep any fumes from causing irritation to your eyes and lungs. Occasionally remove the pot lid and gently stir the fiber, allowing it to absorb the iron evenly. Simmer for 15 to 20 minutes.

Remove the dye pot from the heat, and allow the fiber to cool before washing.

Wash the fiber with pH-neutral soap, and rinse thoroughly to get rid of any remaining iron particles. Hang fiber to dry.

Fig leaves in a stainless steel pot
ready for extraction and iron mordanting.

An old iron garden chair shows rust from exposure to moisture.

IRON AFTERMORDANT OR MODIFIER

Iron is a good aftermordant for darkening or modifying dye color. An iron modifier can be added directly to the dye bath after you've removed it from the heat and before you've added the fiber to the dye bath. Measure the dry weight of your fiber before soaking.

4 ounces (113 g) fiber
2 percent (1/2 teaspoon) iron powder to weight of fiber

Soak the fiber in water for at least 1 hour.

Prepare the dye bath you wish to use, according to any recipe in this book.

Remove the fiber from the soak water, and add it to the dye bath.

Dye the fiber according to the recipe you have chosen. Remove the dye pot from the heat, and let the fiber cool. Remove fiber from the dye bath and hang the fiber to reach room temperature.

Put the iron powder in a cup, add some hot water, and stir to dissolve. To the dye bath you've just used, add the iron solution and stir. The dye bath may be cool at this point, and it's better to have the bath well under the boiling point to avoid breathing vapors. You may notice an immediate change of color for dyes that are especially sensitive to iron.

Place your dyed fiber back into the dye-iron solution. Stir gently so the fiber achieves even coloring. Let the fiber soak in the dye bath for at least 15 to 20 minutes.

Remove the fiber, wash well with pH-neutral soap, and rinse thoroughly. Hang to dry.

IRON MORDANT SOLUTION

You can create an easy iron mordant solution, or iron liquor, by soaking rusty found objects like nails. Once you have created your iron liquor, you can keep it stored indefinitely in a lidded jar for your projects. A little can go a long way. Be sure to label the iron liquor jar. Presoak the already dyed fiber for at least 1 hour before mordanting with the iron liquor.

Large glass jar with a tight lid
Rusty nails or other rusty iron objects
Water
White vinegar

In the jar, place the rusty iron objects. Add 2 parts water to 1 part vinegar to the jar, filling the jar to cover the iron objects. Put the lid on the jar and seal tight. The water will turn to a rusty-orange color in 1 to 2 weeks. You can let your iron mordant liquor sit for as long as you like.

The iron liquor can be used as a mordant by adding it to a stainless steel dye pot, and adding enough water to cover your fibers.

Put the dye pot on the stove. Add presoaked dyed fiber, bring the iron bath to a simmer, 180°F (82°C), and gently simmer for 10 minutes.

Remove the dye pot from the heat, and let the fiber cool. Remove the fiber from the pot, and squeeze excess iron solution back into the dye bath, which can be stored as iron mordant for later.

Thoroughly wash the fiber with pH-neutral soap, and rinse until the water runs clear to remove all iron particles. Hang the fiber to dry.

Making your own iron mordant solution is fun and easy. All you need is rusted iron scraps, white vinegar, and water sealed in a jar, then let time work its magic.

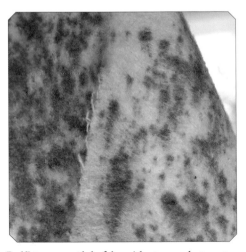

Red Japanese maple leaf dye without a mordant creates a pink, and when splashed with iron yields a rich dark gray.

Plant-Based Mordants

Certain plant materials contain high concentrations of tannic acid, or tannin, which works well as a mordant to bond color to plant-based fiber. Tannin as a mordant, especially in combination with alum, can provide a greater color range with more successful results on most vegetable fibers. Certain tannin-bearing plant materials work especially well as mordants, such as horse chestnuts, pine bark, certain roots, some leaves, acorns, oak galls, pomegranate rind, and some fruits. Among the plant-based mordants, oak galls contain the highest amount of tannic acid. Some tannin substances will bind to the fiber and stay clear, allowing the true color of the dye source to saturate the fiber. But some tannins can alter the color by making it dull, especially if the dyes are yellow, pink, or brown tones.

Acorns, oak galls, pomegranate rind, and certain leaves and bark are just a few excellent sources of plant-based mordants that will brighten your dye color. You can collect acorns and oak galls on the ground under oak trees when they are in season, and store them for later use. You can also buy oak galls from some specialty herb stores.

Shelled acorns can be crushed using a mortar and pestle. Acorns make good dyes since they are an excellent source of tannin.

Try This:
Dip baby booties in softly colored acorn dye.

ACORN DIP-DYED ANGORA BABY BOOTIES

Baby booties made of angora and then dip-dyed in acorn dye and iron make stylish and warm covers for little toes. The soft colors of acorn dye and iron are perfect for these little treasures made from sweater cuffs. In dip-dyeing, only a section of the object is submerged in the dye.

Dip-dyeing with acorns is a fun and easy way to bring seasonal dye color and warmth to tiny toes.

Pomegranate rind makes both a beautiful dye and a natural nontoxic mordant. Pomegranate flowers can also be beautiful additions to your garden.

ACORNS. Acorns can be collected under oak trees in autumn, or you can buy acorn powder from specialty herbal or grocery stores. Grind foraged acorns to a powder, removing the shells, and soak the acorn material in water for several days to get the full color intensity. Acorns create colors from light beiges to grays and teal blues.

OAK GALLS. Oak galls are formed where wasps have laid their eggs on oak tree branches. The galls look like balls sticking to the branch. Galls make an excellent mordant, especially for vegetable fibers, and can be collected from many kinds of trees, especially oak trees (*Quercus* species). Oak galls have extremely high tannin content, which is also found in plant sources like bark and leaves, and is a natural mordant. It enhances the dye color as well as improving colorfastness. Alum can be used to treat fiber with tannin in one or two dye baths to achieve even stronger color results.

POMEGRANATE RIND. The powdered rind, or skin, of the pomegranate (*Punica granatum*) can be used as a tannin mordant, as well as a dye to obtain peachy yellow with alum mordant, and to get gray to moss green with iron mordant. Pomegranate rind was also used as a color source for painting medieval illuminated manuscripts. The age of the fruit affects the color of the dye: the less ripe the fruit, the greener the yellow.

JUNIPER NEEDLES. A natural mordant can be made from the needles of the juniper tree (*Juniperus communis*). Gather the dry branches and burn them over a wide container. Catch only the needle ashes, and add 1 cup of ashes to 2 cups of boiling water. Stir and strain. The liquid is the mordant.

Using juniper needles as a mordant comes from the Navajo tradition. Juniper ashes can be a substitute for alum as a mordant, making the dyes more colorfast and creating brighter shades. Caution: Be careful with this homemade mordant. Since the ashes and water can form a type of lye, which is highly alkaline and can cause burns, use protective measures when working with it.

SUMAC LEAVES. The leaves of sumac (*Rhus* species) are rich in tannin, making them a good natural mordant. When dried, sumac leaves can contain up to 35 percent tannin per weight. Sumac as a mordant brightens and extends colorfastness for most vegetable- based fibers.

USING TANNIN MORDANTS WITH PLANT FIBERS

When using tannin mordants with plant fibers like cotton, linen, or hemp, allow extra time for the process, sometimes up to 2 to 3 days.

{ RECIPE }

BASIC TANNIN MORDANT WITH PLANT FIBER

Two popular sources for making a tannin mordant are oak galls (from *Quercus* species) and sumac leaves (*Rhus* species). This recipe is for oak galls, but you may substitute sumac leaves of the same fiber weight. Work with thoroughly scoured fiber.

4 ounces (113 g) plant fiber
1 ounce (1 teaspoon) powdered oak galls

Soak the fiber overnight in cool water.

Place the oak gall powder in a stainless steel pot with 4 to 6 gallons (16 to 23 l) of water, and stir to dissolve. Bring the solution to a simmer, 180°F (82°C), and simmer for 30 to 60 minutes.

Remove the pot from the heat. Allow the tannin bath to cool down from hot to warm.

Lift the wet fiber out of its soaking pot, and submerge it in the tannin bath. Let it steep from 8 to 24 hours.

Remove the fiber from the tannin bath. Rinse the fiber in lukewarm to cool water. then wash with a pH-neutral soap, rinse again thoroughly, and hang to dry.

{ RECIPE }

ALUM MORDANT WITH TANNIN-TREATED PLANT FIBER

After processing your plant fiber with a tannin bath before dyeing, you may want to use alum as an additional mordant to make your color even brighter. When you have rinsed the fiber of tannin, you can apply an alum premordant once, or twice for even brighter results from your dye. Wear gloves when putting your hands in the alum solution. You can save the leftover alum mordant for later use in a sealed, labeled jar. You can also use iron as an additional mordant after using tannin on your fiber, which will make your dye color darker.

4 ounces (113 g) plant fiber
20 percent (4 teaspoons) alum per fiber weight
6 percent (1 1/2 teaspoons) washing soda per fiber weight

Soak fiber in water for at least 1 hour, or overnight.

After mordanting the fiber in tannin solution and rinsing, hang it to drip while you make the alum mordant solution.

Place the alum and the washing soda into a stainless steel pot half full of water, and stir well to dissolve.

Add more water to the pot, enough to cover the fiber you will be treating, and then add the wet, tannin-treated fiber to the pot.

{ CONTINUED } ·······························➔

ALUM MORDANT WITH TANNIN-TREATED PLANT FIBER (CONT'D.)

Heat the alum solution to the simmering point, 180°F (82°C). Turn off the heat and let the fiber steep for 4 to 8 hours, making sure to stir occasionally so the fiber absorbs the mordant evenly.

Once the fiber has set (achieved maximum effect from the alum mordant), remove the fiber and gently squeeze the mordant solution back into the pot.

Wash with a pH-neutral soap, rinse thoroughly, and hang to dry.

DYEING AND MORDANTING TOGETHER

For a quicker, more energy-efficient method of dyeing and mordanting, you can extract the dye and then add the mordant to the dye bath before adding your fiber. Use the dye recipe of your choice from this book. This method of mordanting and dyeing together is called the all-in-one method.

Wet the fiber and let it soak for at least 1 hour.

Per the dye recipe instructions, extract the dye from the plant material, and strain the plant material from the dye bath. Let the dye bath cool down.

If you are working with a cold-water dye bath, place the appropriate amount of mordant into a cup, add some hot water, and stir to dissolve. If you are working with a hot-water dye bath, place the measured mordant directly into the extracted color in the dye pot and stir well.

If you are working with a cold dye bath per the recipe, put the fiber in the dye bath and let it steep for several hours until the desired shade is reached.

If you are working with a hot dye bath process per the recipe, add the fiber to the dye pot, bring the bath up to a simmer, 180°F (82°C), and simmer for 20 to 30 minutes or until the desired shade has been reached.

Remove the fiber from the dye pot. Wash it gently in lukewarm water with a pH-neutral liquid soap, and rinse well until the water runs clear. Hang to dry.

Pouring your iron and alum mordant baths into the garden can fertilize acid-loving plants with the added minerals.

```
{ RECIPE }

POT-AS-MORDANT

Using an iron, copper, or aluminum pot as a mordanting vessel
is an easy way to make dyeing one step quicker.

    Soak the fiber in water for at least 1 hour.
    Place the fiber in a metal mordanting pot (either iron,
copper, or aluminum) full of water, heat to simmer, and
simmer for 30 to 60 minutes. Turn off the heat, and let the
fiber soak overnight.
    Then dye the fiber according to the dye recipe you choose
in this book.
```

Using Your Pot as a Mordant

Your mordant may also come from the metal of the dye pot you are using. The dye color results will be less scientific, but the experimentation and ease of the pot-as-mordant method can be inspiring. You can stock your dye studio with pots that are made out of these metals, and reserve those pots just for mordanting.

Safe Disposal of Mordants

Mordant baths usually expire when used in correct proportions: the fiber will probably have soaked up all the mordant, so there's no bath liquid to save. Disposing of your mordant needs to be considered thoughtfully. Responsible disposal of your materials is key to sustainable practices. Mordant solutions made with alum, iron, and tannin, if absorbed effectively by the fiber, can be safely poured down the drain with plenty of water, or poured onto the soil in your garden. Cooled alum and iron mordant baths can be poured at the base of acid-loving plants like conifers, mountain laurels, azaleas, hydrangeas, and blueberries. These metallic compounds are often used to fertilize these plants in higher concentrations. Be careful, however, to not disturb the pH balance of your soil or compost pile, by pouring too much acid or alkali into your garden and hurting your plants. So dispose of your mordant in different spots in the garden over time.

Using Modifiers

A modifier can be used after the initial dye process to change the color created on a fiber. Modifiers can also be used to create variegated colors on fabrics. For instance, you can dip a cabbage-dyed piece of fabric in an acid modifier on one end and an alkaline modifier on the other end and get two strikingly different color changes. White vinegar and citric acid are easy acid modifiers to experiment with. Wood ash and baking soda are alkaline modifiers that can also provide modifier results. Iron can also be a modifier when applied after an initial dye bath, to improve the colorfastness of most dye colors and to create darker or more somber color tones. You can also add modifiers directly to certain plant dye baths to change the color before you dye a fiber.

FUGITIVE DYES

Fugitive dyes are dye colors that fade or disappear after time or exposure to light. Turmeric is a good example of a fugitive dye: at first it can be a really bright yellow, then as you wash the fabric and expose it to light, the color will mellow to a warm or muted yellow.

Turmeric is known as a fugitive dye: with exposure to sun and washing, the color will fade from bright yellow to lighter, less saturated shades.

Fugitive dyes can be fascinating: they can give you some short-term but brilliant results, and can be more about the process than the product. Working with fugitive dyes can allow a single garment to become a canvas for many dyeing opportunities. Although the color is not permanent, there is creative benefit to the process.

It's interesting to explore the effects of fugitive dyes. For example, lay a piece of dyed cloth on the ground, and place rocks or other objects on it. Over days, let the sun fade the color away from the fabric, and you'll end up with saturated color patterns in the areas of the textile that were underneath the objects.

OPPOSITE PAGE, ABOVE AND BELOW, LEFT: *Processing leaves for the dye bath can be as simple as taking them off the stem, chopping them, and allowing the plant material to soak.* **OPPOSITE PAGE, CENTER:** *Birch bark is a great dye material to work with. It naturally falls off the tree and is easy to collect.* **OPPOSITE PAGE, RIGHT:** *Bark for dyeing can be collected from felled or pruned trees and branches, and also sometimes from wood shops, neighbors, or public park workers if you just ask.*

PROCESSING LEAVES AND BARK

Leaves and bark can be processed and used easily as dye-producing plant materials. Letting leaves and bark soak over a long period of time can help to coax out the truest colors. Eucalyptus leaves, which can yield a wide range of colors, are a good example to experiment with. Gather the leaves and soak them covered in cold water for 2 or 3 days to create extracted dye.

Processing barks can also be a lengthy process but well worth it. Bark from trees should never be taken straight from the trunk, since that could damage the tree. Wait until the tree has been pruned or felled. Some trees with dye-producing bark, such as birch (*Betula* species), eucalyptus (*Eucalyptus* species), and Pacific madrone (*Arbutus menziesii*), seasonally shed their bark, making it easy to gather the bark as dye material.

DYEING MANY MATERIALS

Plant dyes can be successfully applied to all sorts of natural materials. Experimenting can be fun to see what objects you can color with the dye. Some good materials to experiment with include reeds and other light-colored basketry materials, buttons, shells, leather, and wood. You can also consider simply adding unusual items to the dye bath if they are made of natural materials. White silk shoes or wool clogs can be dyed with natural dyes for some beautiful results. Contrary to the general rule of thumb, sometimes synthetic fibers will soak up natural dyes. So, experimenting with vintage or thrift store finds can provide some interesting results. Just add the object to the dye bath and see what happens.

All sorts of materials can be dyed with botanical colors, even natural objects like shells and sea stars.

MAKE DO AND MEND

During World War II, citizens were encouraged to grow their own produce in home "victory gardens." A slogan was also promoted, "Make Do and Mend," to encourage do-it-yourself activities for taking care of one of our basic material needs, clothing. In the 1940s, it was a common practice, for example, to dye your clothes at home and to use plant sources like cabbage and onionskins for the dyes. In just a few generations, this economical and sustainable mode of kitchen couture has all but disappeared from fashion.

As with cultural and family traditions, recipes for the use of dye plants and dyes are also a cultural treasure. Learning about dye recipes from your family's past or from your local region can lead to joyful discoveries about the symbiosis of food, plants, and clothing that people have shared for generations.

The activities of Make Do and Mend also included hints on washing your clothes, mending holey areas in your knitted garments by knitting them again, creating decorative patches and applying them to rips and tears, redyeing and covering stains in old clothes, and increasing the lifespan of a garment, including how to keep moths and other harmful bugs away using nontoxic natural materials. Make Do and Mend is an awareness movement that has been reborn in our current culture, much like the Do it Yourself (DIY) network. These two concepts are about conservation and creativity with your clothing and textiles, and many Web sites and nonprofit organizations are connected to this movement.

REUSING FABRICS

When choosing a fabric or fiber to dye, you don't need to start with just white. Taking a blue garment and dying it yellow will make it green, giving you a fresh, new garment. And you can get some exciting surprises when you overdye an already patterned floral, plaid, or otherwise printed or woven fabric with a natural dye. Starting with a canvas that is not blank can also open your eyes to the fabric possibilities that await in thrift and secondhand stores or in the back of your closet.

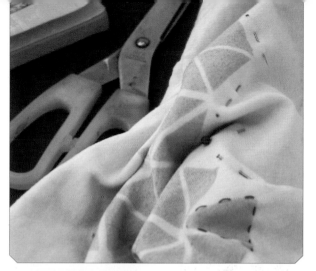

ABOVE: *Think of recycling and repairing before buying new textiles or disposing of old garments. This pre-loved T-shirt is taking on new life after being dyed with tea, and is about to sport a reverse appliqué in a beautiful pattern.*
BELOW: *Taking cuffs from soft old sweaters and making them into baby booties is a fun way to upcycle, or give richer purpose to, textiles. These adorable booties were then dip-dyed in acorn dye and iron (see page 45).*

WASHING and CARING FOR NATURALLY DYED TEXTILES

When people ask me if garments made of natural materials and dyed with natural dyes can be thrown into a washing machine and dryer just like conventional garments, I always say the answer is yes and no. Natural fabrics dyed with natural botanical colors should be cared for as delicates, because they don't do well with harsh care, chemicals, or additives. If you take special care of your naturally dyed garments, they will last longer.

Hand washing your dyed garments and fabrics in cold water and hanging them out to dry are better for the textiles and smarter on our energy resources. Drying your clothes on a clothesline can be an easy, simple Slow Textiles activity. There is nothing more beautiful than a line of clothing drying and blowing in the breeze. You can admire your carefully dyed work and save energy in the process. The mission of the nonprofit organization Project Laundry List is to make air-drying laundry once again acceptable and desirable as a simple and effective way to save energy. Before dryers, the washing was always hung on a clothesline and dried in the sun and breeze. When I was growing up, we had a clothesline, and fabrics smelled sweet and clean from being aired outdoors.

Use ecologically based and biodegradable pH-neutral soap to wash your naturally dyed fibers and fabrics. It does the job and will not alter the integrity of your color or your textile. Using soap that is ecofriendly also will help to keep the water in our streams, lakes, and oceans clean.

Old clothing and linens can be upcycled by dyeing them in baths of black walnut hull and mint.

NATURAL BLEACHES

You may occasionally need to bleach your naturally dyed textiles prior to dyeing to remove stains or kill germs and bacteria. Common household chlorine bleach is very harsh and I don't advise using it on your botanically dyed natural fibers. Not only will it fade the color of the dye, but it can be caustic to the skin and eyes and emits dangerous fumes that are bad for the lungs.

Sunshine is a natural bleach and a natural sterilizer. Hanging clothes on a line in the sun will freshen the textiles and whiten them over time. With colored garments, be careful not to leave them in the sun too long, or they may fade.

Lemon juice is a natural, nontoxic bleach that can take out stains without other harmful side effects. The citric acid in lemon also acts as a powerful disinfectant and sanitizer. Caution: lemon can very effectively remove iron from fiber, so remember this when working with iron as a mordant with certain plant dyes. You can, in fact, create some interesting patterning effects with lemon placed purposefully on iron-mordanted fabric.

To use lemon juice as a stain remover on natural white textiles, pour straight lemon juice onto the stain. Then rub the area with salt. Place the garment in the sun for several hours. Hand wash with a pH-neutral soap, rinse thoroughly, and hang to dry.

Instead of adding chlorine bleach to your white laundry, you can add lemon juice. But keep lemon juice away from your naturally dyed textiles, unless you just want to remove a stain.

The juice of lemons can remove stains from white textiles and iron spots in your naturally dyed clothing.

USING PLANT DYES TO PROTECT YOUR TEXTILES FROM INSECTS

Dyeing a fabric or garment with plant materials like lavender or bay laurel can provide natural antiseptic qualities that will not only make your textiles smell wonderful but it will also infuse your textile with a natural repellant against moths and other insects. The same smell that we consider a pleasant fragrance is a natural repellant to such pests. Dyeing textiles with these plant materials is a desirable alternative to toxic methods like mothballs for protecting vulnerable natural fibers like wool, silk, and linen from insect attack. And you'll know that your textile will be safely protected for a long time.

Lavender, that heavenly fragrant plant, when used as a dye can also repel insects from your natural fibers.

LAVENDER DYE

Dyeing fiber with the flowers of lavender (*Lavandula* species) creates a shade of pale, antiqued gray-pink with no mordant, a slightly brighter shade of beige with alum as a mordant, and a teal-gray with iron as an aftermordant. Using the leaves and stems creates yellows with alum to greens and grays with iron added. Among natural fibers, silk and wool will hold a more saturated color from lavender. With proper mordanting, linens and cottons can be used; plant-based fibers may achieve a color that is slightly less bright with no mordant compared to animal fibers, but can still retain a pleasant fragrance. Use the mordanting recipes appropriate for your fiber (pages 40-49). If you would like to use lavender to protect the textile as a natural antiseptic, rather than as a color, no mordant is necessary.

Use equal weight of the lavender plant material to dry weight of the fiber. This recipe uses heat to extract the color from the lavender. You can also choose to use the cold-water solar or sun-tea extraction processes.

4 ounces (113 g) fiber
4 ounces (113 g) lavender plant
material (flowers, stems, leaves)

Soak the fiber in clear lukewarm water for at least 1 hour, or overnight for better absorption of color.

Chop the lavender plant material and place it in a dye pot with enough water to cover the fiber you will be dyeing. With the dye pot on a burner, bring the water to a boil, then lower the temperature and let the bath simmer, 180°F (82°C), for 30 to 40 minutes. Turn off the heat, and let the dye bath cool to room temperature. You can let the plant material steep in the dye pot overnight for deeper, darker color results.

Using a strainer, scoop out the dye material from the dye bath.

Place the wet fiber or fabric in the room-temperature dye bath. Over a burner bring the dye bath to a simmer, and let the fiber steep in the dye pot for at least 20 minutes. Remove the fiber.

Wash the fiber gently with a pH-neutral soap. Rinse thoroughly. Hang to dry.

LAVENDER DRESS

This wool dress has been dyed with lavender flowers, stems, and leaves to give it a subtle yellow color and to protect it from moths. Lavender flowers complement it beautifully.

This angora wool child's dress was dyed with lavender and alum, creating a sweet color and sweet smell that will protect and care for this precious textile.

Chapter 2

Cooking with Color

Inspiring Recipes for Nontoxic Color

It is exciting to realize just how many plants you can use to create natural dyes. Experimenting with various plant sources for producing color can be rewarding and even awe-inspiring. Red cabbage (*Brassica oleracea*), for example, can create nontoxic, multidimensional shades of blue and purple. Over the years, as my interest in working with plants has grown, I have become a much better dyer and a much better cook, almost simultaneously. Learning to cook from scratch is a great way to sharpen your skills for working with naturally dyes, and vice versa.

Dyeing different fabrics with one cabbage dye bath can result in many different color tones.

KITCHEN COUTURE

Some of the easiest natural dyes for the beginning dyer to work with are in your kitchen cabinet. They are fun, nontoxic natural dye materials to get you started with the world of color.

Turmeric

Turmeric is a tropical plant that yields an orange-yellow spice from its dried, ground root. Turmeric dye creates a bright yellow. You can use the ground turmeric root available in powdered form in the spice section of your market. Or if you live in a tropical area, you can easily grow the turmeric plant for dye material; using freshly grown turmeric root will create an even stronger dye color. You process turmeric root either by cutting it into small pieces, then grinding or pureeing it, to create a bright and satisfying dye.

As an easy and rewarding beginning project, consider dyeing an old piece of natural fabric or a seldom-worn cotton, silk, or wool garment you have in your house. There's something magical about transforming a familiar object into something stunning and new with a dramatic color change. Examples could be a piece of reclaimed linen fabric that you turn into a vibrant yellow tablecloth, an old white wool sweater that is freshened with a bright yellow hue, or a plain cotton shopping bag you want to make more colorful.

And don't forget: you can use the dye bath for multiple projects at once.

ABOVE: *Turmeric powder can be found in your kitchen or market, and makes a beautiful yellow dye.* **BELOW:** *Turmeric dye without a mordant is nontoxic and safe to place your hands in, since it is a food. Just watch for your hands turning yellow as well.*

TURMERIC DYE

The root of the turmeric plant (Cur-cuma longa) creates strong colors, from bright yellow with no mordant to dark green with an iron modifier. Cold water works well for turmeric; for darker and more orange shades, heat can be applied. Turmeric is a great dye for beginners as it works equally well on animal- or plant-based fibers with or without a mordant.

4 ounces (113 g) fiber
2 ounces (56 g) dry powdered turmeric root

Presoak your fiber in cool water for at least 1 hour. Use enough water to cover your fiber.

In a cup, dissolve the turmeric, add some cold water, and stir to dissolve.

Fill a dye pot with enough cold water to cover your fiber so it can move freely. Add the turmeric solution and stir to mix.

Add your presoaked fiber to the dye bath. Put the dye pot on a burner, and bring the water to a simmer, 180°F (82°C). Simmer the fiber for 20 to 30 minutes, occasionally stirring gently so the fiber absorbs the dye evenly.

When your fiber has reached the desired shade, remove it, wash it thoroughly with pH-neutral soap, and rinse thoroughly until the water runs clear. Hang to dry.

Try This:

Warm up a wool sweater, a cotton shopping bag, a tablecloth, and fabric gift wrap with turmeric dye.

TURMERIC-DYED WOOL SWEATER

A preowned wool sweater has been given new life with a vibrant yellow turmeric dye.

Turmeric offers a quick and easy way to spice up your closet.

TURMERIC-DYED SHOPPING BAG

A turmeric-dyed shopping bag is not only fun to make; it's also a naturally sustainable choice. Making your own shopping bag eliminates using bags made from depleted resources and toxic dye materials, and you always need more bags to bring with you to the market. You can create your own bright yellow shopping bag with any cotton-based fiber, since turmeric takes well to plant-based fibers. Turmeric is a perfect choice for doing a dye project with children, since it's nontoxic and so easy to work with. Watching the color bond to the fiber can be lots of fun.

A reusable grocery bag that you have dyed yourself with a kitchen spice will help you feel even more connected to your food.

A woven cotton shopping bag gets treated with a bright new color from turmeric.

The shopping bag has been sitting in a bowl in the sun being dyed by turmeric.

SUMMER PICNIC TABLECLOTH

If you love food and design, there is nothing more satisfying than connecting with both the spices you use in food preparation and those you use to dye the tablecloth you put your meal on. Using colorful spices such as turmeric, you'll have fun as the dyer, and you'll get bright dyes that will connect your picnic guests to the process.

{ CONTINUED } ·······················➤

The edges of this linen tablecloth have been dipped into turmeric dye, creating a bright yellow.

As you dip each section, avoid letting it drip or streak; allow enough time for the dye bath to be hand-squeezed so it won't run. If you are working with a large piece of cloth, fold the fabric in half or in quarters, to dip each end evenly.

Gently squeeze extra rinse water out of the dyed fabric, and make sure the water runs clear.

A spiced-up tablecloth can be fashioned from any fabric made of any natural fiber. You can find old white cotton to work with or get more experimental. With already printed vintage tablecloth fabrics, like plaids or floral patterns, you can drench them in a new yellow hue. Dyeing just the edges of a cotton tablecloth with bright yellow turmeric dye can be striking, creating a nice bright border around your delicious picnic spread.

TURMERIC GIFT WRAP

Cloth-wrapping, or furoshiki as it is known in Japan where this environmentally friendly technique originated, allows you to wrap almost anything regardless of shape or size. With folding methods similar to those of origami, you can use naturally dyed cloth for gift wrapping, food shopping, or as beautiful decor.

Your finished turmeric dip-dyed picnic tablecloth will be sure to add some creative spice to any occasion.

Gorgeous cloth gift wrap can be made from turmeric-dyed fabric scraps. Stitching colorful knots into the fabric adds another dimension.

COMPOST TO COLOR
and COLOR TO COMPOST

Many kitchen waste products can be used for dyeing, before you place them on the compost pile. These dye sources are especially fun and easy for the beginning dyer, since they are readily available. In the following three recipes, you'll learn how to make vibrant dyes from familiar cooking by-products: onionskins, red cabbage, and black walnut hulls.

Onionskins

Onionskins (from *Allium* species) are a longstanding, nontoxic culinary by-product used for dyeing. Onionskins do not require using a mordant to obtain nice color. You can get an even bigger supply of onionskins at the grocery store or farmers market, by asking vendors for their extra onionskins; they are often happy to see their waste material go to good purposes.

Onionskins work very well with solar dyeing, a simple and energy-efficient way to create a dye bath. Place a large pot of onionskins and water inside your home-built solar oven, cover with a clear lid, and place in the sun to soak for a few hours until you get the color results you want. You can also simply place onionskins in a large jar of water to sit in the sun, just like making sun tea.

ABOVE: *Making dye from kitchen scraps like onionskins can be a fun process between cooking and the compost pile. Yellow onionskins can create rich reds and burnt oranges.* **BELOW:** *Red onionskins can create yellow and orange shades.*

ONIONSKIN DYE

The peelings from onions create wonderful
dye colors. Yellow onionskins create shades
of burnt orange and gold. Red onionskins
create bright yellows and yellow-greens.
To dye protein fiber such as wool or silk,
follow mordanting instructions for these
fibers (Basic Alum Mordant with Wool, page
40; Basic Alum Mordant with Silk, page
40; or Iron Aftermordant or Modifier, page
43). To dye a plant-based fiber like cotton or linen, pretreat the fiber appropriately with washing and mordanting (see Iron
Aftermordant or Modifier, page 43; Basic
Tannin Mordant with Plant Fiber, page 47;
or Alum Mordant with Tannin-Treated Plant
Fiber, page 47).

4 ounces (113 g) fiber
4 ounces (113 g) onionskins

Soak the fiber in water for at least
1 hour.

Place onionskins in a dye pot with
enough water to cover the fiber you will be
dyeing.

Place the dye pot on a burner, bring to
a boil, turn the heat down to a simmer, and
let the onionskins simmer, 180°F (82°C), for
10 to 15 minutes, or until the water has
turned a rich deep color and the onionskins
have become clear. Turn off the heat.

With a strainer, scoop the onionskins
from the dye bath. Add the fiber to the dye
bath, and bring the bath to simmer again.
Simmer for at least 10 minutes, or until
the desired color has been reached. Your
fabric can also be left to steep in the
dye bath overnight or for a longer period
of time to achieve darker, more saturated
color.

Wash the fiber with a pH-neutral soap,
rinse thoroughly, and hang to dry.

Try This:

Add warm tones to the trim for a fabric bag using yellow onionskins.

BAG WITH ONIONSKIN SILK-HEMP TRIM

Yellow onionskin–dyed silk-hemp fabric adorns the edge of this small bag woven of nettle fiber.

Plant color can make an interesting trim on just about anything.

Red Cabbage

Red cabbage (*Brassica oleracea*) is a surprising natural color source that can produce vibrant colors from lavender to brilliant blue. I love working with cabbage: it's such an ordinary everyday vegetable that you wouldn't expect it to yield such beautiful colors.

The leaves of the red cabbage are usually dark red-purple because of the anthocyanin pigment in the plant, but cabbage will change color depending on the pH value of the soil. When growing in acidic soils, the cabbage leaves will become more reddish, while alkaline soil will make them more greenish-yellow, and therefore the same cabbage plant can be different colors in different regions. Furthermore, the juice of red cabbage can be used as a homemade pH indicator: the juice will turn red in acid and blue in alkaline solutions.

Growing your own garden for food and color can be an extremely rewarding experience. These red cabbages will be ready for my dye pot in two to three months.

ABOVE: *A red cabbage plant in its beginning stages of growth has striking coloration.* **BELOW:** *A fully grown red cabbage is ready for color experiments in the dye pot.*

RED CABBAGE DYE

You can experiment with the cabbage dye bath by adding salt to get a more blue shade and lemon or another acid modifier to get more pink colors. An average cabbage will weigh about 2 pounds. Cut up the cabbage to get the most dye color from the leaves.
If you would like to dye protein fiber like wool or silk, follow the mordant instructions for your fabric on pages 40–49. To dye a plant-based fiber like cotton or linen, use Alum Mordant with Tannin-Treated Plant Fiber, page 47. For best results without a mordant, use animal fibers.

1 pound (454 g) fiber

1 pound (454 g) red cabbage, cut into 1-inch chunks

2 ounces (59 ml) lemon juice or vinegar, optional

1/2 cup salt (60 g) to 8 quarts water, optional

Soak the fiber you will be dyeing in water for at least 1 hour, or overnight.
Fill a dye pot with enough water to cover the fabric you will be dyeing. Place the pot on a burner and bring the water to a simmer, 180°F (82°C).

Put the cabbage in the pot, bring the water back up to a simmer, and simmer for 20 minutes, or until the leaves begin to lose their original color and become a light pale pink and blue.

Remove the dye pot from the heat. With a strainer, scoop out the cabbage from the dye bath. Return the dye pot to the burner, and bring the dye to a simmer.

Add the presoaked fiber to the dye bath. Bring the dye bath back up to a simmer, and simmer gently for 20 to 30 minutes.

At this point, if you want to modify the warm purple-lavender dye color, you can stir in some acid (vinegar or lemon juice) to create a pink shade, or you can get dark blue by stirring some salt into the dye bath to make it more alkaline. Let the fabric simmer until the desired shade is achieved. The fabric can also be left overnight for more saturated color. Wash the dyed fiber with a pH-neutral soap. Rinse thoroughly. Hang to dry.

ABOVE: *Different fibers turn different shades of purple-blue in a cabbage dye bath.* **CENTER:** *Adding an acid (vinegar or alum) or alkaline (salt) modifier to the red cabbage dye bath can vary the final color.* **BELOW:** *A cabbage leaf after simmering in water turns a translucent pink. The blue and purple color have gone into the dye bath.*

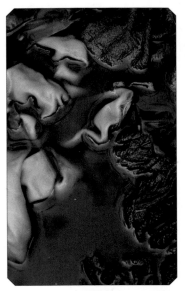

ABOVE: *Letting the fabric soak in the dye bath overnight will result in the fiber absorbing darker shades.* **CENTER:** *When your fabric has reached the color you desire, remove it from the dye bath and wash, rinse, and hang dry.* **BELOW:** *Watching your fabric dry is a way to admire your work.*

Try This:

Let a silk wrap and a wool knitted hat share the smoky hues of a red cabbage dye bath.

RED CABBAGE HAT AND WRAP

Dye baths can be used for many projects at once. A reclaimed silk wrap was dyed with red cabbage dye in the same pot as the dip-dyed organic wool knitted hat.

Red cabbage is a super easy dye to work with and can create beautiful wintry blues to offset any wardrobe.

Black Walnut Hulls

The hulls of black walnuts, from a tree (*Juglans nigra*) native to the central East Coast forests of North America, are among the easiest natural plant dye materials to work with. You can gather black walnuts from the ground under the trees in September and October if you live in a region where they grow. Black walnuts are a treasured, delicious ingredient in many culinary recipes. Crack the nuts, save the nutmeats for eating and cooking, and crush the hulls into powder. Black walnut powder can also be found in markets and health food stores.

Black walnut hulls yield shades of cream, light browns, and deep browns. The dye can be processed with a low water temperature or by the sun tea method. The dye does not require a mordant to make strong color, but adding alum is helpful for achieving richer shades of brown. With an iron modifier, black walnut hulls can create rich beiges and browns, and even blacks.

{ RECIPE }

BLACK WALNUT HULL DYE

This black walnut hull dye recipe uses no mordant and will produce light brown. If you add alum, the dye will be a golden brown. On wool and silk fibers, black walnut hull dye can produce especially rich, warm tones if you follow mordanting instructions for wool (pages 40–41) or silk (page 41). If you want to dye darker colors on plant-based fiber like cotton or linen, use Alum Mordant with Tannin-Treated Plant Fiber (page 47) or an iron aftermordant (page 43).

4 ounces (113 g) dry fiber

2 ounces (56 g) powdered black walnut hulls

1 tablespoon alum, optional

Soak the fiber at least 1 hour in water, or overnight.

In a dye pot, put enough water to cover your fiber, add the walnut hull powder, and stir to dissolve.

Bring the water to a boil, and turn down to a simmer, 180°F (82°C). Add the wet fiber, and simmer for at least 20 minutes or until the desired shade is achieved.

Wash the fiber with a pH-neutral soap in warm to cool water. Rinse thoroughly, and hang to dry.

Try This:
Create subtle patterns on silk pillow covers
with black walnut hull dye.

BLACK WALNUT HULL–DYED SHIBORI PILLOW COVERS

Peace silk pillow covers colored with black walnut hull dye create a
warm and elegant accent to the décor of any room. Peace silk walnut-
dyed pillow covers can be easily patterned with shibori (Japanese for
resist dyed), an ancient method of creating pattern in fabric, which is
still used in cultures on every continent on the planet. Shibori patterns
can be made by many different resist methods of dyeing cloth, including binding, stitching, folding, twisting, or compressing, before it goes
into the dye bath.

   Working with shibori can be an easy, delightful way to create color
patterns on your fabric. All you need to do is fold your fabric in your
chosen way, secure it so it will stay folded, and immerse it in the dye
bath long enough for the dye to bond on the fabric. After you have
dyed the fabric, and washed and rinsed it, then open your fabric to
reveal the repeated pattern. Instructions for two simple shibori resist-dye
methods follow.

SHIBORI FOLD-AND-CLAMP TECHNIQUE

Folding your fabric back and forth and then binding it with clamps
before you dye it, as in this recipe, can result in some intriguing gridlike
patterns. You can also fold it back and forth in a triangle shape for stunning diamond effects. Here's what you do:

   Fold your dry fabric back and forth like a fan. Then fold it back and
forth from the long way to create a square.

   Bind your fabric square with short sticks using two to clamp and
bind each side securely with twine or rubber bands so the clamps will
not come loose in the dye bath.

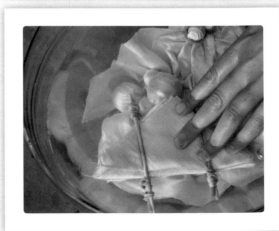

Soak your bound fabric in water for at least 1 hour or preferably overnight.

Add your bound fabric to a dye bath of your choice in this book. Let the fabric simmer in the dye bath for at least 20 minutes, or enough time to let the fabric become saturated by the dye bath.

Remove the bound fabric from the dye bath. While it is still folded and bound, rinse in clear water. Unclamp the fabric, and admire the beautiful pattern you have made.

Wash the fabric with pH-neutral soap, rinse thoroughly, and hang to dry.

SHIBORI WRAP-RESIST TECHNIQUE

In this simple shibori method, you use stones (or you can even use peach pits), and you wrap your fabric around the stone, binding it securely with string or rubber bands. This easy technique can create intriguing graphic patterns on your textiles.

Wrap your dry fabric around a stone, bind it securely, and soak it in water for at least 1 hour, or preferably overnight.

Remove the bound fabric from the water and place it into a dye bath of your choice from this book.

Follow the instructions for dyeing, as you would for any fabric. When the desired color is achieved, remove the bound fabric from the dye bath.

Rinse the fabric-wrapped stone.

Unwrap the shibori and admire the pattern you have made.

Wash the fabric with a pH-neutral soap, rinse thoroughly, and hang to dry.

Two pillow covers were patterned using two different shibori techniques and dyed with black walnut hull.

MAKING YOUR OWN COMPOST

When working with your dyeing materials in an ecofriendly manner, there is no better way to begin and end than with the compost pile.

Just as with cooking, composting your dye plant materials is a great a way to reuse them. Composting is an excellent practice to add much needed nutrients to your soil. Plant material on the compost pile breaks down surprisingly quickly, yielding dark, rich, fluffy organic material, just like you would find on the forest floor. And creating compost from your kitchen waste and dyeing scraps is a very satisfying process. It is a direct way to get in rhythm with the needs and results of your garden.

Composting can be done anywhere, and is a valuable contribution to the earth's ecological balance. Whether you have a large property in a rural area or you have a small patch in an urban environment or even live in an apartment, composting is fun and easy. Composting in urban areas helps to restore or replace worn-out or contaminated soils for gardens and urban food systems. You can share responsibilities and scraps for a composting project with roommates or neighbors. Urban compost systems are appearing in former vacant lots, and even on rooftops and at school and community buildings. Some cities areas have a composting program that will collect your waste for you and do all the work.

Composting can be as simple as a backyard heap. You can also compost indoors or out in a garbage can or a worm bin. Composting is a perfect way to recycle the botanical waste from your dye projects. Examples of everyday things that can be composted are:

- [ ] cardboard rolls
- [ ] clean paper
- [ ] coffee grounds and filters
- [ ] cotton rags
- [ ] dryer and vacuum cleaner lint
- [ ] eggshells
- [ ] fireplace ashes
- [ ] fruits and vegetables
- [ ] garden trimmings
- [ ] grass clippings
- [ ] hair and fur
- [ ] hay and straw
- [ ] houseplants
- [ ] leaves
- [ ] nutshells
- [ ] sawdust
- [ ] shredded newspaper
- [ ] tea bags
- [ ] wood chips
- [ ] wool rags

To maintain your compost pile, you should turn it occasionally with a pitchfork or shovel to introduce oxygen needed for the microbes that work on decomposing the organic material. How often you turn the compost can vary from every 3 days to every 6 weeks. The more often you turn it, the faster it will break down.

When your compost has broken down, it will have a sweet earthy smell. It can take anywhere from a few weeks to a year for compost material to become usable as a soil amendment. Sprinkle the compost among your garden plants and work it into the soil to replenish nutrients and enhance soil texture.

ABOVE: *Composting your kitchen and dye waste to create garden soil can be a fascinating process.*
BELOW: *Prunings can be peeled for bark and lichen to test in the dye pot.*

Compost can include food scraps, yard waste and garden prunings, and even biodegradable natural fibers like wool and cotton.

Dye, then Compost

Wait! Before you throw that kitchen waste on the compost pile, remember that many plant materials can create wonderful dye colors. Cooking with some of the plant and dyeing with the rest is a great way to use the whole plant. In addition to onionskins, cabbage leaves, and black walnut hulls, some other examples are:

AVOCADO SKINS can be saved and used to create dye color, making a fleshy pink color with no mordant.

CARROT TOPS create a wonderful shade of yellow.

TEA BAGS AND LEFTOVER TEA are very simple means of dyeing all types of natural fabrics and fibers.

COFFEE GROUNDS can be very useful in the composting process, especially if your soil is very alkaline and contains dense clay. Coffee grounds can amend the soil back to a healthy pH level, providing a happy spot for growing new plants. Coffee grounds are also thrown away at coffee houses every day. You could ask your neighborhood barista if you may collect the grounds for your dye projects.

These yarns have been dyed with kitchen waste: coffee, blackberries, onionskins, and avocado rinds.

ABOVE: *Just one week's worth of kitchen waste dyed these vibrant yarns.*
CENTER: *Tea bags can be easy to use as a natural dye with cotton fabric.*
BELOW: *Coffee beans can be reused for a dye that creates beautiful rich browns on all types of fiber.*

COFFEE DYE

Roasted coffee beans (*Coffea arabica*) create rich brown dye. The darker the coffee bean has been roasted, the darker the dye and the more intense brown you will be able to achieve. Espresso beans are roasted darker than regular beans. For even darker coffee dye, you can steep the coffee and grounds for an extended period in a light-proof, lidded container, so it can age without growing mold. You can also save your coffee grounds to use with warm neutral colors; the grounds can yield a warm beige that can soften bright colors and create an antiqued tone. Depending on how dark the coffee roast is and the delicacy of the fiber you are using, you can use hot-water extraction or cold-water extraction. No mordant is necessary when using coffee dye on both animal- and plant-based fibers, although the addition of a mordant can improve both light and washfastness and extend the range of rich browns.

Create a coffee dye bath dark enough to color your fiber the desired shade of brown. In the dye pot, the bath should be deep enough to allow the fiber to move around freely.

Add your soaked fiber to the dye pot. Slowly heat the fiber in the coffee bath to simmering point, 180°F (82°C), and simmer for 15 or 20 minutes. Turn off the heat and let fiber steep until the desired shade has been reached. Leave the fiber overnight if you want a deep brown color.

Wash the fiber with pH-neutral soap. Rinse thoroughly. Hang to dry.

Coffee dyeing is both easy and economical. It's a wonderful way to reuse—you can start with the grounds that remain after your own morning coffee.

COFFEE OR TEA SHIRT

In true "make do and mend" fashion, this T-shirt was dyed with saved coffee grounds. Softly colored and softly styled, the shirt is a rich cream-brown.

Coffee dyes cotton very well, making it an excellent choice for dyeing T-shirts. If you prefer tea to coffee, it works just as well!

This espresso-dyed shirt was organic and fair trade from coffee cup to naturally dyed cloth.

Chapter 3

Harvesting Hues

Gathering and Growing Your Own Color

One of the reasons I started working with natural dyes was so that I could make my own nontoxic color from plants that connected me to my local environment. Considering what is in season is applicable to your food, but also to other plant products, such as fibers and dyes. Whether on a large-scale agricultural level or for the artisan dyer, knowing when your plants are in season can make a big difference for many reasons.

When harvesting natural plant materials for dye colors, it is important to gather fresh plants at their peak in order to get the brightness of dye color you are hoping to achieve. Dried herbs can also be used, but they will result in less brilliant hues.

ABOVE: *Participating with nature means noticing its patterns and recognizing that there are many components to a diverse and healthy ecosystem.*

OPPOSITE PAGE, ABOVE LEFT: *Horsetail, considered a living fossil, has been in existence for over 100 million years. The leaves create a soft light green or yellow dye.* **OPPOSITE PAGE, ABOVE CENTER:** *This knitted wool textile has been dyed with horsetail, creating a glowing yellow.*

BELOW: *This deep silvery gray dye is made from Japanese maple leaves and iron. The tannin in the leaves helps to create an interesting chemical change in the color.*

LOCAL COLOR

Knowing what plants are native in your area is a great way to learn about your bioregion. It can also help you identify invasive weeds in your garden, which you can pull for use in the dye pot and to prevent further spreading of those non-native plants. Native plants have evolved over a long period of time in a specific region. They are the plants that Native peoples of a particular region knew and depended on for food, clothing, and shelter.

Working with native plants is often a win-win situation for multiple reasons. First, it is often easier to identify native plants and their uses in your particular area, since historical societies, local plant experts, and local libraries may already have information on how these plants have been used and cultivated in the region.

The benefits of native plants extend beyond human usage issues. Native plants are often already adapted to regional weather and pests, making these plants optimal and energy efficient to grow. As the California Native Plant Society says, "Native plants are those that have co-evolved with animals, fungi, and microbes to form a complex network of relationships. They are the foundation of our native ecosystems, or natural communities. Knowing what is native to your region can be beneficial for weather patterns, for energy usage in watering, and for more deeply connecting with ethnobotany, nature, and nurture of the area in which you live."

The advantages of growing native plants and working with them as dye sources include:

- ☐ **They save water.** Many native plants need minimal water beyond rainfall that occurs naturally.

- ☐ **They are low maintenance.** Native plants take less care in the garden. You spend less time pruning, weeding, and watering.

- ☐ **They naturally resist pests.** Native plants have built-in resilience to pests and many diseases in your region. Most pesticides are toxic and also kill beneficial insects. Eliminating pesticide use in your garden is a wiser way to grow plants, and will lessen toxic runoff that ends up in our soil, creeks, and local watersheds.

- ☐ **Native plants attract wildlife.** In nature's symbiotic system, native plants, butterflies, insects, birds, and many other animals work together to assure that the whole will thrive. Wildlife in a region thrive best with native plants. Putting native plants in your garden and encouraging public and private land sites in your community to do the same can provide a much needed wildlife corridor to nearby remaining wildlands in the region.

OPPOSITE PAGE, ABOVE: *A meadow of native plants in bloom can be a stunning sight.* **OPPOSITE PAGE, BELOW:** *The blossoms of sour grass create a bright yellow dye.*

Knowing what is in season, as well as recognizing when you are increasing your carbon footprint by buying things that are not local or seasonal, are important means to deeper ecological understanding of your dye materials. Mark your calendar with when wild plant materials will be available, when you are planning to dye samples for a project. Just like a chef working on a menu in advance, you want to make sure your materials will be available.

ECOLITERACY AND THE DESIGN PROCESS

Ecoliteracy is a term that refers to understanding our ecological landscape. Ecoliteracy is the ability to comprehend the language of nature, its interconnections, and its limits. And the idea of ecoliteracy is directly related to my interest in harvesting natural plants for dye materials.

Much of what has become problematic in our modern lives is related to our having forgotten how to connect with simple rhythms of nature. We are often out of sync with the seasons, what plants grow in our bioregions, and how to recognize them by name. The gift of learning to identify plants of this world, the pleasure of growing your own food or useful plants, how to cook, or how to create a color palette from soil to studio are concepts directly related to ecoliteracy. Spending time outside allows you to build a relationship with nature, to know the plants that are harmful, and to recognize those that are useful, as well as those that are common, local, and in season.

With natural dyeing, you become directly involved with the plant and its life cycle. When you are working with the natural world, you're constantly aware that you are often working on nature's schedule, not just your own. Knowing when plants are in season is especially important for dye sources that are foraged and collected from wild sources. Planning to dye with the seasons means that your projects can be successfully started and completed while the desired materials are available. Paying attention to nature and to how nature designs, whether it is through brilliance of color or through form and function, can be an invaluable source of design inspiration and innovation in your own creative process.

TIPS FOR GATHERING AND USING FRESH PLANT MATERIAL FOR DYES

Helpful tools for plant gathering:

- ☐ garden gloves
- ☐ pruning shears
- ☐ baskets for collecting plants
- ☐ a good sun hat

Gathering materials:

- ☐ Gather fresh flowers when they have just come into bloom.
- ☐ Pick and use berries for dyes when they are ripe.
- ☐ Harvest most roots in the fall.
- ☐ Collect leaves and bark in the spring.

Processing soft plant materials to make a dye bath:

- ☐ When using just flowers for dyeing, separate flower petals from other plant material.
- ☐ If using leaves for dyeing, chop them so they yield more dye.
- ☐ If using fruit, chop the fruit.
- ☐ For most wild-harvested plants, use equal weight dyestuff to fiber you are dyeing.
- ☐ Place dyestuff in a large dye pot, and cover with enough water to submerge the plant material as well as the fiber you will be dyeing.
- ☐ Bring water to a boil and simmer for 30 minutes or the recommended time.
- ☐ Strain the plant material from the dye bath.

Processing hard plant materials (roots, nuts, and barks) for a dye bath:

- ☐ Break up or chop roots.
- ☐ Break up nut hulls and bark.
- ☐ Use equal weight of nut hulls, roots, or bark per weight of fiber.
- ☐ Soak nut hulls, roots, or bark overnight in 2 gallons cold water, or enough to cover the fiber you wish to dye. Strain out the plant material from the dye bath.
- ☐ For roots, place in a dye pot with another 2 gallons of water, and simmer roots for 1 hour. Strain the plant material from the dye bath.

Sour grass

Sour grass (*Oxalis pes-caprae*, also known as Bermuda buttercup), a wild plant in the wood sorrel family, is found around the world. It has cloverlike leaves and bright yellow buttercuplike flowers. Characteristic of many members of genus *Oxalis*, sour grass plants contain oxalic acid, which gives the parts of the plant a pleasant sour taste. Children love to chew the stalks of sour grass. The dye works well with silk, wool, and cotton, creating a brightly saturated summery yellow.

In many countries, sour grass blossoms are truly a sign of spring. Where I live in California, sour grass season follows the winter rains, and fresh flowers are usually available from late February to early May, when they wither as the dry hot weather begins. Gathering sour grass flowers and leaves while they are robust and creating your color when the dye plant is fresh is the best way to assure that you will get a bright, vibrant yellow.

Sour grass—a sure sign of spring—can be processed by chopping the flowers, stems, and leaves and placing the material in a dye bath.

{ RECIPE }

SOUR GRASS DYE

The flowers and leaves of sour grass are a great source of yellow dye. You can extract dye from sour grass with cold water, or for quicker results, you can use heat. Because sour grass contains oxalic acid, which is a natural mordant, it's not necessary to use an additional mordant to achieve bright yellow results with sour grass dye on animal- or plant-based fibers, although the addition of a mordant can extend light- and washfastness. Sour grass is also sensitive to modifiers, so that adding an alkaline modifier, such as baking soda, can create a bright orange color instead of bright yellow.

4 ounces (113 g) fiber
4 ounces (113 g) sour grass flowers
and leaves

Presoak the fiber cool water for at least 1 hour.

Chop the sour grass flowers and leaves into small pieces. Put the sour grass in a pot full of water, enough to cover your fiber.

If using the hot-water dye method, bring the water to a simmer, 180°F (82°C), and simmer the plant material for 15 to 20 minutes, or until the plant parts lose their color. With a strainer, scoop out the plant material from the dye bath.

Place the wetted fiber in the dye bath, and simmer for 15 minutes, and remove. Or steep overnight to achieve more saturated color.

If using the cold-water dye method, place the sour grass in a large water-filled glass jar big enough to hold your fiber or in large open bowl. Place the jar in a sunny spot until the water

{ CONTINUED } ·······························➤

SOUR GRASS DYE (CONT'D.)

starts to turn yellow. With a strainer, scoop the plant material from the dye bath. Place your fiber in the sour grass dye and let it steep for as long as it takes to get the desired shade.

Lift fiber from the dye bath, and wash with pH-neutral soap. Rinse thoroughly, and hang to dry.

As sour grass simmers, it loses its vibrant colors and the dye bath turns bright yellow.

Try This:
Use sour grass dye for a luminescent yellow scarf.

SOUR GRASS COTTON SCARF

Fabric dyed with sour grass can be bright yellow and even have a green tint, depending on how the light hits it. This cotton is dyed a vibrant yellow. It would make a lovely scarf.

Sour grass weeds from your garden or neighborhood can create an almost fluorescent green-yellow dye.

Fennel

A wonderful plant to use in dyeing is fennel (*Foeniculum vulgare*). A perennial that grows wild in many parts of the world, fennel is used as both an herb and a dye plant. Fennel can be found in the summer in the San Francisco Bay Area where I live, alongside the road, in vacant lots, and in dry riverbeds. Fennel is an excellent natural dye source for creating shades of bright yellow and green.

{ RECIPE }

FENNEL DYE

Fennel-dye material from plant stems, leaves, and flowers yields a bright yellow. Fennel creates a gorgeous yellow green on wool or silk fiber with an alum premordant; with an iron modifier, it yields a deep forest green. For the mordant recipes, see Basic Alum Mordant with Wool, pages 40–41; Basic Alum Mordant with Silk, page 41; and Iron Aftermordant or Modifier, page 43. For plant-based fibers, fennel binds best with a tannin premordant (Basic Tannin Mordant with Plant Fiber, page 47) and then alum (Alum Mordant with Tannin-Treated Plant Fiber, page 47).

4 ounces (113 g) fiber

4 ounces (113 g) fennel leaves, stalks, and flowers

Process the fiber with an alum premordant, per recipe directions.

Soak the premordanted fiber in water for at least 1 hour.

Chop the fennel material, and place it in a pot full of enough water to cover your fiber. Bring water to a simmer, 180°F (82°C), and simmer for 20 minutes. Turn off the heat and let the dye bath cool.

Place the premordanted, wetted fiber into the dye pot, and bring the dye bath back up to a simmer. Simmer for 15 to 20 minutes. For more saturated color, let the fiber steep overnight. While simmering and steeping, weight the fiber with something heavy (like an old plate) to keep the fiber submerged and able to absorb the dye color evenly.

Remove the fiber from dye bath. Gently wash with pH-neutral soap, rinse thoroughly, and hang to dry.

FENNEL-DYED BRIDESMAID DRESSES

If you are planning a wedding, a great idea is to let your bridesmaids choose their own style of dress in a white color. Although the dresses may be different styles, dyeing them all with the same unique plant color provides a gorgeous and unusual way of creating a cohesive look in the bridal party. I advise that the dress fabrics contain silk, not only because it's a great fabric for a dressy occasion, but also because silk readily takes most natural dyes.

If your wedding is outdoors, the bridesmaid dresses will have even more of an impact, since natural dyes often vibrate in natural light because the color is composed of complex molecules that interact with the colors of the landscape. Wild-harvested fennel blooms can also make a bright addition to the wedding bouquets, nicely coordinating the dress color source with the flowers at the wedding. At any wedding or special event, you can use favorite plants from your neighborhood, garden, or region as a way of adding even more meaning and beauty to your celebration.

TIP: If dyeing garments for a special occasion like a wedding, you may want to gently iron or steam-press them after dyeing. Do not take naturally dyed garments to a dry cleaner, since the cleaning processes and chemicals are too harsh and can cause some unfortunate changes to your dresses.

LEFT: *Foraged fennel makes a beautiful dye, and the flowers can be featured in a wedding centerpiece or bridesmaid bouquet.* **RIGHT:** *Bridesmaids wear dresses dyed with fennel collected from my San Francisco Mission neighborhood.*

GROWING YOUR OWN DYE PLANTS

In addition to collecting and harvesting wild color, growing your own dye plants is an ideal way to have a close relationship with your dye material. Working in your garden, whether beside your house, on a rooftop, or in pots in your apartment, can provide a full soil-to-studio natural dye experience.

By growing your own materials and supporting your local economy, you build sustainability into your dyeing practice from start to finish.

Cultivating color from scratch is a partnership with your plants. Identifying which plants you would like to work with for dye colors and deciding how to integrate them into your own garden can be an intriguing departure from gardening as usual. Growing dye plants yourself can give you a deeper aesthetic connection with your garden design. Once you begin to read the ecological landscape through plants and their purpose, your mind can open to creative new garden layouts and concepts.

You can grow your own color. These young onion seedlings are ready to go into the ground.

LIMITS BUILD CREATIVITY

Something that I am continually grateful for as an artist and designer is that I have the opportunity to work small, to learn from my mistakes, and to grow organically. Taking small steps helps us to understand the greater whole from artisanry to industry.

When dyeing with natural plants, you can gain tremendous ecological insight in the most unexpected ways from working closely with the source of your materials. By collecting seasonal leaves from valuable dye plants in the autumn, you can turn them into dye color as well as using them for garden mulch. Mulch moderates soil temperature and moisture by retaining heat and supporting beneficial plant growth, and it also minimizes your gardening labor.

Working seasonally, with what you forage or what you grow yourself, naturally affirms the bigger picture of ecological limitations. To have a sustainable dye practice, you cannot take from nature without giving back. This is especially true of growing your own plants. A little work goes a very long way in assuring that your crops will thrive.

DESIGNING YOUR DYE GARDEN

You can plant dye plants specifically for color, or you can choose plants for food that have by-products that can be used for dyes. In the dye garden planning process, it's helpful to know how long it takes for your plants to mature and when they will be ready to harvest for use in projects.

A vegetable garden can yield food as well as dye materials like carrot tops and onionskins.

When pondering which dye plants to plant in your garden, I suggest beginning with some local, native plants. The ways Native peoples have used local plants through history have been extensively documented, so you can easily find information on the dyes native plants can create. And native plants are often easier to grow and care for because they are acclimated to your particular region's climate, soil, and even the insects and animals.

I have often found that vegetables grown in very healthy soil rich with nutrients will create the brightest color. This had been proved to me again and again as I have worked with organic or biodynamic plants versus those grown in less healthy conditions. The best cabbage I ever used for dyeing was grown on my uncle's biodynamic farm where there are lots of nutrients in the soil. The biodynamic growing method emphasizes a balanced relationship of the soil, plants, and animals as a self-nourishing system. Supporting organics, whether you are growing the plants yourself or supporting the livelihood of others, will not only assure the best color results in the dye pot, but also will make for a healthier user experience.

Raised Dye Beds

In many urban environments, raised beds are favored because they are economical, ecologically sound, and easy to care for. Raised beds allow you to plant a garden in a small piece of land or on a rooftop. With small raised beds, it is easier to create and maintain healthy soil, and to plant and care for your plants. And in raised beds, the soil warms up more easily, causing plants to germinate and grow quickly. Small raised beds are easy to tend, to harvest, and to water.

A spiral garden design is a great way to grow your culinary, medicinal, and dye plants in a small space.

Raised beds are usually simple to make; you can even salvage scrap wood for constructing them. Making a raised bed can be as easy as nailing four wide boards together in a box shape and filling them with good soil. Raised beds can be any size, but they are usually long and narrow, so you can reach any plants in the bed. Remember to site your raised bed in a spot where it will get full sun exposure during most of the day. Arrange the plants so that the short ones are in front of the tall ones, with regard to the sun's rays. so that all the plants get plenty of sunlight.

A Spiral Dye Garden

A unique way of creating a raised-bed garden is by making it a spiral garden. A spiral garden is a round garden made from a spiral of rocks that winds upward, enclosing the soil and warming and dehumidifying it. And since you build the garden upward with spiraled terraces, you can grow lots of plants in a small space. Spiral dye gardens can also be quite fun to have on a school ground or in the community, since they add both practicality and creativity to the garden landscape.

For the spiral garden base, establish a flat site with full sun exposure that measures 4 by 4 by 2 feet (1.2 by 1.2 by 0.6 m). Your finished round spiral garden will be about 3 feet (1 m) high. A good combination of multipurpose dye-producing plants for your garden could include 1 each of rosemary, sage, chamomile, mint, and purple basil. Also get 2 to 4 young plants each of sorrel, spinach, and carrots. Purchase seeds of calendula, nasturtium, and borage, and sprinkle them throughout the spiral garden around the plants. The materials you will need to collect and the instructions for building the garden follow.

1 cubic yard soil, fertile mixture of topsoil, compost, and sand

20 rocks, ranging from orange size to grapefruit size

15 to 20 plants

Use a garden hose to form a circle on the ground where you want the garden. Dig a circular trench around the hose circle, making the trench as wide as the largest rocks you collected and about 4 inches (10 cm) deep. Remove the hose. Make sure the garden base is stable—the rocks in the base circle need to be securely set in the trench. If the rocks are loose, the garden may later collapse. Place the rocks 2 to 4 inches (5 to 10 cm) deep, as close together as possible, and pack dirt around them so that each rock is almost

buried and stays rooted when you try to move it. Once you have the first course of rocks set, put dirt inside the circle to create a round bed that is level with the rock border. Use the end of a hand tool or a stick to stamp the soil until firm.

Make a second layer of rocks, and then spiral the rocks inward and upward, filling in with dirt to create a level surface. Use smaller rocks as you approach the top, making sure to stamp the soil until firm.

To design the layout of your plants, place them (still in their pots) on your spiral to decide on spacing. Research the plants' growing habits, so you'll know which plants will do well next to another and which plants need more room. Dye plants that are large or need plenty of space, for instance, should be placed at the top of the garden spiral, whereas cascading plants should be placed next to the rocks, so they can scramble over them. Dye plants like mint need lots of room to spread, so planting them around the base of the spiral is usually a good idea.

Water all the plants before removing them from their pots. Start planting at the top of the spiral. Use a trowel to dig a hole slightly deeper and wider than your dye plant's root ball. Place the plant in the hole, and fill with soil around the plant, firmly pressing the dirt down around the plant's roots.

When you've finishing planting, thoroughly and gently water your dye garden spiral. Water the spiral once a week during the first summer to help the herbs to get established. Once your dye plants are established, you should only have to water them in droughtlike conditions.

Plants that Delight the Senses and the Dye Pot

As you design your fiber and dye garden, think about what makes the most sense for your needs, both for usage as well as for your particular climate and garden space. Perhaps create a natural dye garden that contains your favorite colors, both in the plants you grow and in the colors that you want to dye. Color can be an inspiring design principle for how you plan and plant your garden. You could think of your garden as a woven textile with patches of many colors, and look for dye-producing plants that will lift your spirits when you look at them. Envision every step of the garden planning process as a way of being inspired, whether it is through texture, pattern, or color. Perhaps you want to have a food garden, with fruit trees included, so you can eat the fruit and use the by-products as dye sources. If you love to cook and you love to dye, you may want to plan a garden filled with both food-producing and dye-producing plants so you can satisfy both of your passions, cooking and dyeing.

Many plants can be used as dye sources after they are used for beauty. After your colorful cut flowers have graced your room, take them from their vases before they wither and make dyes from them. For example, yellow daffodil flowers create shades of yellows and greens; all colors (except white) of dahlia flowers create yellows, oranges, and greens, and dahlia leaves create shades of green; deep red and pink hollyhock flowers make deep purples and pinks; and red hibiscus flowers create blues, pinks, and purples.

Some flowers are good for the dye pot and are also wondrously fragrant. When growing or harvesting flowers, enjoy their delightful scents as cut flowers in a vase before putting them in the dye pot for color. A few examples are:

- ☐ Jasmine (*Jasminum officinale*) makes light yellows and pale greens.
- ☐ Rose hips (*Rosa* species) create a rosy-beige, or a steel-gray with an iron modifier.
- ☐ Lavender (*Lavandula angustifolia*) creates shades from light beige to cool purple-gray.
- ☐ Rosemary (*Rosmarinus officinalis*) will make greens to browns.

Daffodils make a beautiful yellow-green dye. Handle the flowers with care, since the sap can be toxic.

Dye Plants for Medicines and Spirits

Some plants that are used for dyeing are also considered medicinal, and can be used as traditional herbal remedies, including: calendula is used for soothing skin irritations and minor abrasions; mint is used to treat stomach aches and chest pain, and is a natural breath freshener; and elderberries can relieve flu and colds and help keep your immunity boosted. Consider planting a garden that includes some of these herbs, along with your dye plants:

- [ ] Comfrey (*Symphytum officinale*) leaves create shades of light to deep greens.
- [ ] St John's wort (*Hypericum perforatum*) flowers can achieve light browns and yellows to pink and green.
- [ ] Nettle (*Urtica* species) leaves make beige, yellow, and many shades of green.
- [ ] Elderberry (*Sambucus nigra*) fruit yields shades of purple, dark blue, and gray.

You can also enjoy your garden by making spirits from some of the harvest. What could be more fun than creating a spirited beverage from your dye plants? You can make wine from elderberries, juniper berries are a traditional ingredient in gin, and hops are used to make beer.

ABOVE: *Brilliant dahlia flowers yield stunning colors in the dye pot.*
BELOW: *Rose hips can be used to create a steely gray with an iron modifier. The red petals came from the same bush as the rose hips.*

OPPOSITE PAGE, ABOVE: *You can make your own patterned fabric by pressing or beating flowers and plant parts directly into the cloth.* **OPPOSITE PAGE, BELOW:** *Nasturtiums can create a bold color pattern when pressed into cloth. This nasturtium is printed onto acorn-and-iron–dyed silk.*

Bringing the Outside In

Alternative ways to cultivate your own color sources, no matter where you live, are in window boxes and indoor pots. Having attractive dye plants just outside your window and planted in pots throughout your rooms are great ways to enhance your living space. Some examples are:

☐ Bamboo (*Bambusa* species) can easily be grown indoors. Trimmed or fallen leaves and branches from your plant can go straight to the dye pot for beautiful golden yellows and creams, and with an iron modifier you'll get a deep forest green.

☐ California poppies (*Eschscholzia californica*) grow easily in window boxes, and the roots and flowers can be used for bright yellow dyes.

☐ Herbs grow well in window boxes, and you can harvest part of the plant for culinary uses and part for the dye pot. Examples are purple basil (*Ocimum basilicum* var. *purpurascens*) leaves, mint (*Mentha* species) leaves, and dyer's chamomile (*Anthemis tinctoria*) leaves and flowers.

Another way of bringing the outside in is to use your favorite plants or flowers as starting points for many natural dye projects for your interior spaces. Many of us have strong associations with outdoor environments that inspire us or plants we love. Designing textiles based on your favorite plants or landscapes is an interesting way to work with dyes.

What better way to create yardage than from your plants? I have a lot of fun using the trimmings from overgrown flowers and foliage in my garden to create a colorful tribute in my textiles. Some methods of extracting pigment from plants can be can be surprisingly easy and direct.

Hapa-zome, a technique named by Australian natural dyer India Flint, is based on a Japanese method of pressing plant parts against fabric to create imprints. You simply put a leaf or petal between two layers of fabric and pound the fabric to get colorful pattern.

Nasturtiums (*Tropaeolum majus*) flowers can be printed onto silk fabric using a stone and a block of wood to press the flowers' pigment into the cloth. Nasturtiums stems and leaves printed into fabric create a beautiful bright green impression.

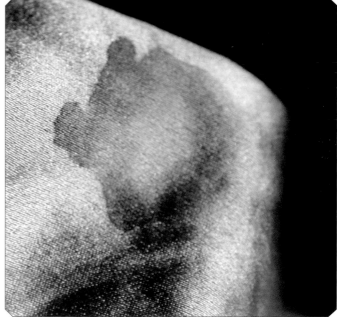

{ CONTINUED } ----------------➤

Try experimenting with printing different kinds of plants onto your fabric. Some color impressions may remain for a while, some will fade quickly. Test what works by washing, rinsing, and drying your dyed samples and let them hang out in the sun to see how rapidly the color fades from the cloth. You can also use other methods of pressing the pigment from dye-producing flowers and leaves onto fabric, like using a rolling pin or pressing in a vise. Being inventive with the process can lead to surprising results.

The Fig Tree

Telling a story through the dye plants you use can also be another tool for designing. Plants often have rich stories of how they have been used throughout the centuries. There are special plants among almost every community and culture. Your friends will be enthralled when you tell them the various traditional stories about your fabric's color source. The fig tree, for example, may be one of the oldest domesticated plants in the world, dating back many thousands of years in the Middle East. You may recall that the fig leaf was one of the earliest articles of clothing, in the story of Adam and Eve. The fruit is delicious and the leaves yield wonderful bright shades of yellow and green.

Fig leaves produce a bright yellow gold on silk and wool.

FIG LEAF DYE

Fig leaves can create rich yellow with an alum mordant and verdant green with an iron mordant. You may have a fig tree in your garden, or perhaps your neighbor does and won't mind letting you have some of its leaves. Harvest fig leaves in the late summer to mid-autumn when they have reached their full size. Do not use the fig stems as dye material; they contain a sticky white sap that can be an irritant to your skin and lungs. Fig leaf dye works well on both plant and animal fibers that have been premordanted with alum, which will create longer lasting, brighter color. This recipe is for silk ribbon, an animal fiber. For an alum premordant, see Basic Alum Mordant with Silk, page 41. For an iron premordant, see Basic Iron Mordant with Animal Fiber, page 42. To dye plant-based fibers with fig leaf dye, wash and pretreat the fabric appropriately and use a mordant (Basic Tannin Mordant with Plant Fiber and Alum Mordant with Tannin-Treated Plant Fiber, page 47).

4 ounces (113 g) fiber
4 ounces (113 g) fig leaves

Soak the premordanted fiber in water for at least 1 hour.

Chop the fig leaves, which allows more dye color to come out of the plant material. Avoid touching sap from stems.

Put the leaves in a dye pot with enough water to cover the fiber you will be dyeing, and bring to a simmer, 180°F (82°C), and simmer for 15 to 20 minutes or until the leaves turn brown and the water turns bright yellow. Turn off the heat. Strain the leaves from the dye bath. Let the dye bath cool.

Add the premordanted wetted fiber to the dye bath. Simmer for 40 minutes, then remove the fiber, or turn off heat and let it steep overnight.

Wash the fiber with pH-neutral soap, rinse thoroughly, and hang to dry.

FIG LEAF-DYED
SILK RIBBON NAPKIN TIES

Your chosen dye material can inspire a whole dinner,
from menu to table setting. Whether you are working with figs, olives, cabbage, onionskins, fennel, or
blackberries, dye plants can bring beauty to any feast.
When you are serving fresh figs, to get the dinner conversation going, embellish some simple linen napkins
by creating fig-dyed silk ribbon, and use it to wrap
around, thread through, or stitch and embroider the
napkins.

Silk ribbon dyed with fig and tied around dinner napkins can be a colorful accent to a meal.

WONDERFUL WEEDS

Some of the most invasive plants in your garden can be sources of both color and beauty before getting sent to the compost pile. It is an open secret for any aspiring textile designer, lover of color, or appreciator of plants that so-called weeds can hold unique dye color properties.

The most common weeds, such as dandelions, can be used for dye, food, and cut flowers for indoor pleasure. Just like with any botanical source, having weeds in a vase and looking closely at them can be a powerful way to generate creative ideas. Just a few common weeds and the beautiful dye colors they produce are:

☐ Blackberry (*Rubus fruticosus*) fruit: light pink to dark blue-gray.

☐ Chamomile (*Anthemis tinctoria*) flowers: yellow, bright golds, gray-greens, deep greens; leaves and stalks: light green to bright green and gray-green.

☐ Dandelions (*Taraxacum officinale*) flowers and leaves: yellows and greens.

☐ Black-eyed Susan (*Rudbeckia hirta*) flowers, leaves, stems: yellows, dusky browns, dark greens.

☐ Fennel (*Foeniculum vulgare*) flowers, leaves, stems: bright yellows to dark greens.

☐ Ground elder (*Aegopodium podagraria*) leaves: yellows and greens.

☐ Goldenrod (*Solidago canadensis*) plant tops and flowers: bright yellows to golds and greens.

☐ Horsestail (*Equisetum arvense*) plant parts: light pink to salmon and browns.

☐ Nettle (*Urtica* species) leaves and plant tops in early summer: creams, gray-blues, dark greens; plant tops in late summer: yellow-creams, beige, brown.

☐ Queen Anne's lace (*Daucus carota*) plant tops: yellows, dusky blue-grays, vibrant dark greens.

☐ Scotch broom, or common broom (*Cytisus scoparius*) plant parts: minty greens, yellows.

☐ Sorrel (*Rumex acetosa*) leaves: pale yellows, greens; roots, rich reddish-browns.

☐ Sour grass (*Oxalis pes-caprae*) flowers and plant parts, bright yellows to golds, deep greens.

By learning more about the plants in your region, you will be able to identify the weeds that can create fantastic dye color. Do research on the weeds that show up in your garden. Often times you can learn very interesting facts about where the plants came from, how they got there, and why they grow well in your soil, which will lead you to a better understanding of your garden's ecosystem.

In northern California, many of these dye-producing weeds are also invasive species—plants that are not indigenous and can harm the balance of nature. Rather than just using these plants for dye materials and ultimately putting them on your compost pile, you might want to form a partnership with a native plant society to learn which plants are invasive and what you can do about them to help restore native habitats.

LEFT: *Dandelions, a common garden weed, provide nutritious foraged greens as well as good dye colors. The flowers and leaves make beautiful shades of yellow and green.*
ABOVE: *Dandelion sun tea creates a beautiful slow extraction dye.*

COLLECTING and SHARING DYE RESOURCES

Touring your neighborhood to learn where the acorns fall and the dandelion weeds come up through the sidewalks will help you to consider the landscape in a whole new light. Foraging when done with proper assessment of availability can be extremely rewarding. Foraging can also be a satisfying way of getting to know your neighbors. By connecting with your community and sharing resources, you'll learn what plant materials, such as fallen fruit, weeds, or newly pruned branches, may be in abundance in your area.

Setting up exchanges with friends and neighbors is also an excellent way to extend the dyer's palette. Projects such as Forage Oakland, in California, create fruit and edible plant exchanges, so that neighbors meet and redistribute extra vegetables and fallen fruit to put them to good use. You could start a project like this for finding and sharing useful dye plants in your neighborhood, or for collecting the weeds and waste from others' yards to create your own beautiful textiles. Urban foraging groups are a wonderful means to learn about and share the many ways you can use your plants of choice.

Ethical Harvesting

Foraging in nature should be done with care, to keep both you and the environment safe. It's important to practice what is called ethical harvesting, or making sure you follow all standards related to collecting plant materials from the landscape; be mindful of the limits in your local ecology and to know when plant materials are vulnerable to overgathering. In any bioregion, overgathering can throw off the balance of food sources and habitats for wildlife as well as cause problems for other plants, water systems, and species composition. Few people realize that it is seldom permissible to dig up whole plants from the wild: even public lands usually don't allow that. So you will be collecting plant materials and whole plants only with special permission. Some of the issues to consider when foraging for dye plant material are:

☐ Know each plant material you are harvesting, since many plants have poisonous look-a-likes. Know each plant by sight, and know their characteristics. Do your research, and talk with plant experts, whether they are herbalists, botanists, or other natural dyers in your region who know their plant sources.

☐ Make sure that you are foraging on land that is open to harvesting, and that you have asked permission of the owner or caretaker before collecting.

☐ Choose material from plants that appear healthy and in abundance. If collecting whole plants, leave the strongest to encourage a future supply. Leave plants on the top of hillsides because they will seed downslope. When gathering plant parts, shake to redistribute any seeds.

☐ Never gather endangered species. Go to Web sites like United Plant Savers for a list of endangered and threatened plants.

☐ Harvest less than one-third of naturalized plants or native flowers and leaves and only in abundant stands. If possible, harvest only the part of the plant needed for dyeing. Remember that disturbing the root system can kill the whole plant.

☐ Avoid foraging close to main roads, parking lots, in commercially sprayed areas (most agricultural crop land), and near old houses that could be contaminated with lead and other harmful materials. Avoid collecting in unfamiliar vacant lots or fields, near lawns that have been treated chemically, or downstream from factories or agribusinesses that do not have sustainable practices.

STACKING FUNCTIONS

Often times the natural dyer will use parts of plants that a food forager would not, which makes for more sustainable practices, because all parts of the plant are being used. Aim for "stacking functions," or getting as many different uses as you can, from the plants you use for dyeing.

Growing a tree is a good example of a sustainable practice that can provide stacking functions: a tree can offer shade, fruit, dye material, a home for native wildlife, and beauty, and when it falls, it can provide heat for your home or it can go back into the soil as nutrients.

Growing fruit trees can create an ongoing engagement with the natural world. Your fruit trees will attract desired wildlife, like birds. Some fruit-bearing trees you may already have in your yard that can also produce vibrant dye colors include apple, fig, pear, plum, peach, persimmon, and olive.

Many professionals work with plants that have by-products that you can use as dye material. Becoming friends with a local chef, florist, arborist, or herbalist can be very beneficial to the natural dyer.

Olive branches gathered after pruning can make a colorful dye bath.

LEFT: *Freshly harvested black olives create gorgeous dyes from light salmon pink to teal, depending on the mordant used.* **CENTER:** *Olives can be gathered and cured for delicious eating.* **RIGHT:** *Just like cooking, preparing dyes can be a process full of enjoyment.*

The Olive Tree

Plant an olive tree (*Olea europea*) and you have a wonderful dye source for stacking functions. Olives can be cured as nutritious food, and olive oil has long been a valuable food and herbal remedy. The olive branch, known as a symbol of peace, holds powerful medicinal qualities, and olive leaves were once considered a cure for malaria. The olive tree, besides providing habitat for birds, is one of the most beautiful trees in the landscape and can give decades of pleasure to viewers. Both the leaves and fruit of the olive tree create lovely dye colors.

If you are fortunate enough to have an olive tree in your garden, you will be able to use both the fruit and the leaves for dye materials. Olive fruit thrives with plenty of sunlight, and so you'll want to learn how to prune your olive tree to open up the center and allow lots of light to reach the middle of the tree. You will also want to prune your olive tree to allow for the fruit to be reached most easily. There is almost nothing better than being able to reach out and pick fruit right off the tree. You will not want to eat the fresh olives, though; they're very bitter until they are processed.

If you live in a Mediterranean climate where olive grows abundantly, you can easily grow an olive tree or find someone who has one. Olive ranchers will often allow you to purchase freshly picked black olives or leafy branches directly from them.

OLIVE FRUIT DYE

For olive dye, use freshly picked, ripe black
olives. Olive fruit yields a dye color that is a
pale salmon-pink on its own. With an iron modifier, the color turns to dark teal-gray. For teal
shades, place olive-dyed fibers into an iron aftermordant bath as described in this recipe.

Use the whole ripe black olives including
the pits. Processing whole olives by grinding or
chopping takes patience; the whole olives can be
put into the dye pot, but the dye color will not
be as rich. Olives are oily and can have lots of
small particles that can get stuck in fibers, so
strain the dye bath well. You can use cheesecloth
to capture the oils and fine bits of olives. Or
you can pour the bath through a finely woven silk
scarf, and tie up the dye materials inside the
scarf like a tea bag, and let it sit for a while,
for some interesting patterning results. For tips
on dip-dyeing, see Japanese Maple Dip-Dyed Cotton
Sweater Tank on page 111. With plant-based fibers, pretreating with a tannin mordant (page 47)
and then adding an iron modifier (page 43) will
help to extend the color range.

4 ounces (113 g) fiber
4 ounces (113 g) black olives

Soak the fiber in water for at least 1 hour.

Process the olives and their pits by grinding
with a mortar and pestle or by chopping them into
small pieces.

Place the olives into a dye pot with enough
water to cover the fiber you will be dyeing, and
bring to a simmer, 180°F (82°C). Let the dye bath
simmer for 20 minutes. Turn off the heat, and
strain the dye bath thoroughly.

Place your wet fiber into the dye bath and
bring up to a simmer. Simmer for 20 to 40 minutes, stirring occasionally for even dyeing.
Turn off the heat, and let the fiber sit in the
dye bath until the desired shade is reached.
Remove the fiber from the olive dye bath, or let
steep overnight.

Add the iron modifier to the prepared olive
dye bath and stir to distribute. The dye bath
will immediately change color: the pink will turn
to teal.

Add the olive-dyed fiber to the iron modifier bath and let it steep (no heat is necessary)
until the desired shade is reached. For light
shades, steep 2 to 5 minutes; for medium shades,
steep 5 to 20 minutes; for darker shades, steep
30 to 40 minutes or overnight.

Wash fiber with a pH-neutral soap, rinse thoroughly, and hang to dry.

Try This:

Dip an alpaca rug in olive dye, and use olive leaves to dip-dye a wool hat.

OLIVE FRUIT DIP-DYED RUG

The ends of this domestic alpaca rug have been dip-dyed in olive fruit dye and an iron modifier, adding an interesting gray-teal dye to a neutral textile.

Processing olive leaves for a dye bath is a pleasant and "slow" activity.

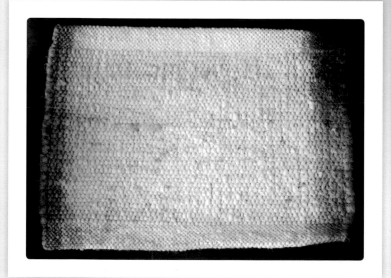

Fresh black olive fruit picked ripe off the tree in the fall can create stunning shades of teal gray-green to accent any natural fiber home décor.

Planting an olive tree can add beauty, food, and shade to your garden.

OLIVE LEAF DYE

The leaves of the olive tree can also be used as a dye source, creating different colors depending on the premordant chosen: from light yellow (no mordant), bright yellow (alum premordant), dark green (iron modifier), and yellow-green (alum premordant and iron modifier). Creating dye from the leaves of your olive tree prunings is a delightful way to make something beautiful out of plant waste. Premordant your fiber using Basic Alum Mordant with Wool, pages 40–41, and/or Iron Aftermordant, page 43. If you want to dye a plant-based fiber like cotton or linen, use Alum Mordant with Tannin-Treated Plant Fiber, page 47.

4 ounces (113 g) premordanted fiber
4 ounces (113 g) olive leaves

Soak the premordanted fiber in water at least 1 hour.

Chop the olive leaves into small pieces.

Put the leaves in a pot full of water, and bring to a simmer. Simmer the leaves until they begin to change color from light blue-silver-green to dark khaki green. Turn off the heat and let the leaves steep overnight. Strain the leaves from the dye bath.

Add the wet, premordanted fiber to the dye bath and bring to a simmer. Simmer for 20 to 30 minutes. If you are satisfied with the color, remove the fiber. If you would like a darker color, let the fiber steep in the dye bath overnight.

Wash the fiber with a pH-neutral soap, rinse thoroughly, and hang to dry.

OLIVE LEAF DIP-DYED HAT

Experimenting with dyes from your garden can be fun, and if you're lucky enough to have an olive tree (or know where to find one), you can make a dye from the leaves. This hat is dip-dyed with olive leaf dye. Follow the directions in the recipe, including premordanting the hat you want to dye.

This wool hat was given new life from some fallen olive branch leaves. Dyeing just the edge of your project can highlight the gorgeous contrast between your natural dye and natural wool.

MAPPING YOUR NEIGHBORHOOD

I enjoy making a seasonal map of places and times of year where I can find good fiber and dye plant material and where I am permitted to forage. Having such a handy visual resource allows me to quickly recall the best places to go and when, to collect botanical dyestuff. Whenever I walk by a tall fennel plant, a yellow-blossomed mustard plant, or a thick blackberry bush overtaking a vacant urban lot or sidewalk, I make a mental note, and at home I add the location and date to my map. Wild plants usually pop up at the same spots every year, even if they die back and disappear during the winter.

Making a map of the dye plants in your neighborhood can also lead to community building among the folks in your neighborhood and between different communities, resulting in taking pride in one's neighborhood or shared open spaces and in differing interests coming together. Making a dye and fiber map can also be a great way of transforming an ordinary landscape into a special shared journey for yourself and for others.

Getting to know the plants in your neighborhood and when leaves and fruit naturally fall creates an immediate personal connection to the local plants that you get to know and enjoy at different seasons throughout the years. In this way natural dyeing can create a magical awareness of circular time. Getting to know plants, seasons, and weather patterns teaches you how to read nature's patterns. Watching the fennel come up along the roadways each year in my region is always a strong marker of time. Watching a tree grow from season to season gives you a closer understanding of the earth's natural processes.

LEFT: *Knowing what trees in your neighborhood drop fruit can lead to beautiful dye colors. This purple yarn was dyed with fallen mulberries.* RIGHT: *Blackberries for dye can be foraged in the wild and even in urban areas. In many areas on the West Coast, blackberries grow in vacant lots.*

LEFT: *Japanese maple leaves can be gathered from sidewalks in autumn in many urban and suburban locations.* **CENTER:** *Soaking and rinsing foraged leaves is a good idea, to remove pollution and dirt before they go into the dye pot.* **RIGHT:** *Japanese maple leaf dye bath smells a bit like hibiscus when the color is first being extracted.*

Japanese Maple

The Japanese maple (*Acer palmatum*) is a tree native to parts of Asia; it also grows well in other temperate regions. The tree is hardy but delicate in form, and is particularly beautiful to look at. It comes in varieties with light green leaves or dark red leaves. The leaves of the light green varieties turn bright golds and reds in the fall before they drop. The leaves of the dark-red varieties turn shades of crimson or bronze in the fall.

I used foraged dark red Japanese maple leaves for dyeing a season of ecoclothing for the San Francisco–based 2009 Mr. Larkin collection. In fall through early spring, I gathered the leaves where they had fallen at the base of two trees in my neighborhood. Japanese maple leaf dye from red leaves creates a beautiful blush pink, and a steel-gray blue with an iron mordant.

CAUTION: When foraging plant materials like fallen leaves, be sure to wash them well in a bowl of cold water with a capful of ecofriendly pH-neutral dish soap liquid before using them, to eliminate the residue of modern life, like pollution and car exhaust, to prevent any contaminants from affecting your dye bath and from getting into your lungs.

LEFT: *The spectacular red of Japanese maple leaf dye can be extracted in either a hot-water or a cold-water bath.* **RIGHT:** *After the dye has cooled, strain it to remove the plant material.*

{ RECIPE }

JAPANESE MAPLE LEAF DYE

Dark red Japanese maple leaves processed without a mordant will dye fiber light pink. Using an iron aftermordant will make your fiber a rich gray with blue undertones. Using the leaves when they turn color in the fall creates stronger shades of pink, and an iron aftermordant (page 43) will lend a warm undertone to the steel-gray. You can use plant- or animal-based fibers equally well with Japanese maple; neither requires a mordant to achieve the soft blush-pink color. The leaves already contain tannin, which allows the color to bind to either type of fiber.

4 ounces (113 g) fiber
4 ounces (113 g) maple leaves

Soak the fiber in water for at least 1 hour.

Chop the maple leaves. Put the leaves into a dye pot and cover with enough water to immerse the fiber you will be dyeing. Bring water to a simmer, 180°F (82°C), and simmer for 30 minutes or until the color disappears from the leaves and the water becomes a rich garnet-red. Turn off the heat, and strain the leaves from the dye bath.

Add your wetted fiber to the dye pot. Bring the solution to a simmer, and simmer for 15 to 20 minutes, or until the fiber has turned a blush pink. Remove the fiber.

If you want your fiber to be a blush pink color, wash it in warm to cool water with pH-neutral soap, rinse well, and hang to dry. If you want to achieve a deep blue-gray, you can use an iron aftermordant. The dye bath will quickly turn to gray or a blue-gray.

Add the dyed fiber to the mordant bath, and let it soak until it becomes fully saturated with color, usually about 10 to 15 minutes. It's not necessary to use heat for the aftermordant to be effective.

Remove the fiber from the mordant bath with nonreactive tongs. Wash the fiber gently with pH-neutral soap, making sure to wash away any iron particles. Rinse fabric thoroughly, and hang to dry.

ABOVE: *The glow of the garnet-hued dye bath is a color experience in itself.* **BELOW:** *Japanese maple leaf dye can be modified from garnet to gray with a pinch of iron powder.*

ABOVE: *Japanese maple leaf dye on the left is a delicate pink with no mordant. The dye bath is a dark, stormy gray with an iron aftermordant.* **BELOW:** *A Japanese maple leaf bath with both wool and silk fibers.*

JAPANESE MAPLE DIP-DYED COTTON SWEATER TANK

In dip-dyeing, you make a section of a garment, textile, or yarn a different color by submerging only that section of the object in the dye.

To dip-dye a cotton knit, prepare your color and let it cool so that you can use it as a cold dye. Gently drop the portion of your garment that you wish to dye into the dye bath. Leave the garment in the bath for 5 to 10 minutes for light color and longer for more saturated pinks. You can continue to hold the garment by hand, making sure the color is even. Or, to allow for longer periods of time and darker coloration, secure the portion you would like to stay clean by attaching it with a clothes pin it to the edge of the pot to keep it out of the dye vat. When the garment has reached your desired shade, carefully remove the dyed portion, wash the garment in cold water with pH-neutral soap, rinse thoroughly, and hang to dry.

LEFT: *The dip-dyeing process with Japanese maple leaf dye can produce color on plant fiber without mordant.*
RIGHT: *This dip-dyed cotton knit sweater was colored with Japanese maple leaf dye for my friend Casey Larkin's Mr. Larkin Spring 2009 collection.*

JAPANESE MAPLE AND IRON LAMP SHADE

Find a lamp shade made of a natural fiber such as cotton or linen. Prepare your Japanese maple leaf dye bath and add 2 percent iron modifier to weight of fiber, stirring to make sure that the iron is fully dissolved into the bath. Let the bath cool to room temperature so as not to melt any glues that may be holding the lamp shade together. Carefully dip part or all of the shade into the dye bath, or get inventive and paint your dye onto the lamp shade, allowing the dye to sit for at least 10 to 15 minutes before rinsing with cold water. Let the lamp shade dry thoroughly.

A natural fiber lamp shade can be dyed with maple leaf dye and an iron aftermordant.

Blackberry

Blackberry (*Rubus fruticosus*) is an inspiring dye plant to work with. The berries, leaves, and stems can be used to create rich color. Like many plants that invite stacking functions, blackberries are also delicious to eat. Blackberry vines can be found in many urban and rural areas, and the berries and leaves are easily foraged in the late summer, early fall.

When gathering blackberry material, you'll want to wear thick gloves and long sleeves for protection, because blackberry bushes have very sharp thorns. And also wear gloves when you prepare the leaves and stems for dyeing.

BLACKBERRY DYE

The berries of the blackberry plant create varying shades of pink, lavender, and dark blue-gray in the dye pot, depending on what mordant you use. Animal-based fibers such as silk or wool take the color much better than plant-based fiber, although you can use either with proper treatment. Prepare your fiber for dyeing by soaking it, whether you want to dye silk ribbon, yardage for sewing your little blackberry dress, or a premade silk dress. To premordant your fabric with alum, see Basic Alum Mordant with Silk (page 41). For an iron modifier, see Iron Aftermordant or Modifier (page 43). For plant-based fiber, a premordant of tannin and alum (Basic Tannin Mordant with Plant Fiber and Alum Mordant with Tannin-Treated Plant Fiber, page 47) is recommended with an iron aftermordant for even darker shades.

4 ounces (113 g) fabric
4 ounces (113 g) blackberries

Premordant your fabric with alum.
Soak the fabric in water for at least 1 hour or overnight.

Crush the blackberries with a mortar and pestle. Place the blackberries in a dye pot with enough water to cover your fiber, and bring to a simmer, 180°F (82°C). Simmer the blackberry dye bath for 20 to 30 minutes, or until the water turns a dark purple-blue. (If you are using a solar oven, heat the blackberry dye bath for approximately 2 hours in full sun, or let it steep overnight.) Turn off the heat, and strain the blackberry parts from the dye bath.

Add your premordanted fabric to the dye bath. Bring the dye bath back up to a simmer, and simmer for 20 to 30 minutes. Remove the dye pot from the heat. Remove the fabric and set aside. (When dyeing plant fibers like cotton, linen, and hemp, leave them in the dye bath overnight or for 1 to 2 days.)

Add an iron modifier and stir vigorously to assure the dye and iron modifier have thoroughly mixed.

Place the dyed fabric back in the dye bath. Let it steep for at least 15 to 20 minutes, or overnight if you want a darker color.

Remove the fabric from the dye bath, wash with pH-neutral soap, rinse thoroughly, and hang to dry.

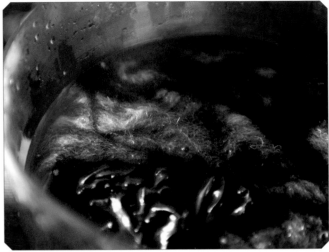

ABOVE LEFT: *A dye bath of blackberries reflects the sun's rays in my outdoor dye studio. Some late summer leaves have drifted into the dye vat, offering a vibrant contrasting yellow.* **ABOVE:** *Wool fleece soaks in a cold deep purple blackberry dye bath.* **LEFT:** *Blackberry dye bath in a glass container.*

BLACKBERRY SILK RIBBON

Vintage items of all types can be dyed. Blackberries add luscious hues to transform your textiles into treasures.

THE LITTLE BLACK[BERRY] DRESS

A white dress from your favorite thrift store or from the back of your closet can be turned into a newfound classic with blackberry dye. Or with sewing skills, you can make your own garment from any blackberry-dyed fabric you choose. A colorful outdoor blackberry dye bath is a wonder to behold.

ABOVE: *Vintage silk ribbon colored with blackberry dye sits next to a plate of foraged wild berries.* **RIGHT:** *A little black(berry) dress couldn't be more iconic, and appropriate for any occasion. Reclaimed silk or wool fabric takes well to blackberry; silk is used for this recipe.*

BLACKBERRY-DYED BEADS

It is exciting to consider how many kinds of material beyond textiles can be dyed with botanical color. I dyed wooden beads with blackberry dye and strung them on a length of fabric cord that I dyed steel-gray. Other beads that work for naturally dyeing are those made of bone or other natural fibers like wool felt or silk. Using your fabric dye scraps for a bead cord can be a great way to accent naturally dyed beads.

Porous wood works well for dyeing beads. You can create a deep rich dye bath without heat, since wood readily absorbs blackberry dye. To crush the ripe blackberries, grind them with a mortar and pestle. Blackberries make a dye that is shades of deep purple and maroon on light-colored wood.

Gather enough blackberries to make a dye bath that will cover your beads. For 1 ounce (28 g) of blackberries, use 4 fluid ounces (118 ml) water.

Crush the blackberries with a mortar and pestle. Put the crushed blackberries in a bowl, add the water, and stir. The dye bath will be thick.

Add the wood beads to the dye bath, submerge them, and soak until they reach the desired color.

Wash the beads with pH-neutral soap, rinse thoroughly, and set out to dry.

ABOVE: *Wooden beads are a fun material to dye and can be used in a variety of projects.* **RIGHT:** *Blackberry-dyed wooden beads, strung on a dyed fabric cord, have a glow about them.*

BLACKBERRY LEAF AND STEM DYE

Blackberry leaves and stems produce shades
of yellow to gray-greens to dark teal-gray,
depending on the mordant used. When you use
alum as a premordant, you will get a vibrant
yellow (see Basic Alum Mordant with Wool,
pages 40-41). When you use iron as a premordant, the colors will be a steely gray-green
(see Basic Iron Mordant with Animal Fiber,
page 42). For plant fibers, use Basic Tannin Mordant with Plant Fiber and Alum Mordant
with Tannin-Treated Plant Fiber, page 47.

4 ounces (113 g) premordanted fiber
4 ounces (113 g) blackberry leaves and stems

Soak the premordanted fiber in water for
at least 1 hour.

Chop the blackberry leaves and stems. Put
the chopped leaves and stems in a dye pot,
and cover with enough water to immerse the
fabric. Let the leaves steep overnight.

Bring leaves and stems to a simmer, 180°F
(82°C), and simmer for 30 minutes, or until
the color disappears from the plant parts and
the water becomes a yellow-green. Turn off
the heat. If you are happy with the color,
strain the leaves from the dye bath. For
darker colors, let the leaves continue to
steep overnight. (If you are using a solar
oven, let the plant material steep in the sun
for 4 to 6 hours, or overnight.)

Add the wetted fiber to the dye pot, and
bring to a simmer. Let the fiber simmer for
15 to 20 minutes, or until the fiber turns a
light green. If you wish a darker shade, let
the fiber steep overnight.

Remove the fiber from the dye pot, wash
it with pH-neutral soap, rinse thoroughly,
and hang to dry.

BLACKBERRY LEAF-DYED SWEATERS

I found two preowned white cashmere sweaters in a
vintage clothing store and dyed them with the same
blackberry leaf dye bath but achieved very different
results. I premordanted one sweater with alum before
putting it in the blackberry leaf dye bath, and it became
bright yellow, and after dyeing the other sweater, I processed it with an iron aftermordant, which turned it teal
gray-green.

You can have fun with this kind of experiment.
Choose an old white sweater from your drawer or pick
up one from the local thrift store. Check the sweater
label: any sweater you use for this dye project should be
100 percent wool or other natural fiber to assure even
dyeing. Follow the blackberry leaf dye recipe; for the
alum aftermordant recipe see Basic Alum Mordant with
Wool, pages 40-41, and for the iron aftermordant recipe
see Basic Iron Mordant with Animal Fiber, page 42.

*Two sweaters dyed with blackberry leaves hang to dry, one treated with an
alum mordant (behind) and one with an iron modifier (front).*

HERBAL ARTS

When you're hooked on natural dyeing, you'll discover that many local markets and health food stores are great places to find dye materials to experiment with. As you delve deeper into the world of natural color, you will also find yourself talking more with herbalists, gardeners, chefs, and anyone else who loves plants.

As you experiment with dyes from plants, you will find that many of these plants are used in the culinary or herbal arts. Medicinal, herbal, and spice-producing plants are often color producing. Herbal sections in shops are great places to find plants that may not be available in your area in bulk or dried form.

Annatto (*Bixa orellana*) is a good example of a dye source you can find in your local health food store. Annatto is a product of the achiote tree that thrives in tropical and semitropical regions of the Americas. Annatto is a pod that contains seeds that create a bright red-orange dye. The seeds ground into powder have been used to produce red food coloring and as a flavoring for many Central and South American cuisines. It was also used as war paint in ancient Mayan culture, and it is used in lipsticks and other cosmetics. In Hawaii, in the neighborhood where my family lives, the annatto plant grows wild. In other locations, you can find annatto in herbal shops or health food stores.

Other plants used for both medicinal and dye reasons include indigo, an ancient source of blue dye, which was used traditionally as a remedy for snake bite; and cabbage was considered an herbal cure-all by the ancient Romans.

Mint

Mint (*Mentha* species) is an aromatic perennial herb, and is used widely as a flavoring herb in cooking and for making tea. Mint thrives in cool, moist climates, and grows rapidly by means of its underground runners. Mint can even become a problem in a garden because it can quickly take over, which makes it an excellent plant for the dye pot.

Mint oil is also used as an environmentally friendly insect repellant to discourage common pests like wasps, hornets, ants, and cockroaches without harming other living beings in the process.

The mint for this dye bath was gathered from my garden, where the determined plant overtook my raised garden beds.

MINT DYE

When gathering mint, harvest just the leaves if you wish the plant to continue to grow, or use the entire plant if you want to thin that area of the garden. The leaves of mint are the strongest color source. Mint smells wonderful while steeping in the dye bath, and creates a mint-green dye color with an iron modifier on both animal and plant fibers (see Iron Aftermordant or Modifier, page 43). Using hot water to process the leaf dye is faster, but you can also use cold water or solar heat if you have more time.

4 ounces (113 g) fiber
4 ounces (113 g) mint leaves

Place the mint leaves in a dye pot of hot water, and steep for about 20 minutes or until the leaves have turned brown and the water is a green-brown color. Strain the leaves from the dye bath.

Add the wetted fiber to the dye bath. Soak the fiber for at least 1 hour, or overnight, to achieve the color you wish. Remove the fiber and set aside.

Prepare an iron modifier and add it to the dye bath per instructions.

Return the fiber to the dye bath, and let it steep until it reaches the desired shade. For a lighter green, steep for about 5 minutes; for darker gray-greens, steep for at least 20 minutes.

Wash the fiber with a pH-neutral soap, rinse thoroughly, and hang to dry.

Try This:

Dye silk ribbon or a felted laptop case (see page 144) with mint.

MINT SILK RIBBON

Wide silk ribbon can be dyed with mint to reach this surprisingly deep teal color.

Dyeing natural fiber ribbons with deeply saturated plant color can accent an abundance of artisan projects.

St John's Wort

St John's wort (*Hypericum perforatum*) is a yellow-flowering perennial indigenous to Europe. The plant has been introduced in many temperate regions of the world and grows wild in many open fields and meadows. Flowers can be picked in midsummer, and bring the brightest shades of yellow when used fresh and put straight into the dye pot. St John's wort has been used for centuries as an herbal antidepressant.

St John's wort is considered to be a noxious weed in some regions, which means that it is a plant that is growing out of its native region, and is considered injurious to pubic health, agriculture, recreation, wildlife, or property. So check local regulations before you grow it in your garden.

The flowers, leaves, and stems of St John's wort have been used as a dye to create many colors. When mixed together, the plant flowers, leaves, and stems create a warm brown. At your local herbalist, you can find St John's wort plant tops in dried form. When growing your own plants, you can pick just the flowers.

Try This:

Create an array of colors for a silk throw and wool yarn with St John's wort flowers.

ST JOHN'S WORT DYED SILK THROW

A cozy silk throw dyed with the warm colors of St John's wort is sure to make anyone happy. You can knit, weave, or buy an undyed silk throw to use as a blank canvas. This recipe uses fiber that has been premordanted with alum, and uses the flowers of St John's wort for the dye. To premordant the throw, see Basic Alum Mordant with Silk, page 41. If using a plant-based fiber, follow instructions for tannin and alum premordants for plant fibers on page 47.

12 ounces (340 g) premordanted silk or wool throw

12 ounces (340 g) St John's wort flowers

Premordant the throw in alum.

Soak premordanted throw in water for at least 1 hour.

Place the flowers in enough water to cover your throw, bring to a simmer, 180°F (82°C), and simmer for 20 to 40 minutes, or until the dye turns bright red. Strain the flowers from the dye bath.

To make the St John's wort dye bath, put the flowers in a dye pot with enough water to cover the yarn, and place the pot on the stove. Bring the water to a simmer, and simmer until the dye turns bright red, about 20 minutes. Turn off the heat. Strain the flowers from the dye liquid. Let the dye bath cool to room temperature.

Put the premordanted, wetted throw in the St

John's Wort dye bath, and simmer for 15 to 20 minutes, or until the throw turns a green-gold. Remove the throw from the dye bath.

Wash in pH-neutral soap, rinse thoroughly, and hang to dry.

ST JOHN'S WORT-DYED WOOL YARN

This project uses the flowers of St John's wort, which yield colors from green to maroon, red, and yellow, depending on the mordant method used. Use 4 skeins of scoured wool yarn, 2 that have been premordanted with alum (see Basic Alum Mordant with Wool, page 40-41) and 2 skeins that have not been treated with mordant. Use fresh flowers from the plant, which will have the seemingly magical ability to produce four different shades in wool yarn, depending on processing methods.

**4 skeins wool yarn, 1 pound (454 g) total
or 4 ounces (113 g) each
1 pound (454 g) St John's wort flowers**

Soak the wool yarn in cool water for at least 1 hour.

To make the St John's wort dye bath, put the flowers in a dye pot with enough water to cover the yarn, and place the pot on the stove. Bring the water to a simmer, 180°F (82°C), and simmer until the dye turns bright red, about 20 minutes. Turn off the heat. Strain the flowers from the dye liquid. Let the dye bath cool to room temperature.

To the dye pot, add 1 skein of wool yarn that has been premordanted with alum, and simmer for 15 minutes until the fabric turns green. Remove the skein from the dye bath and set aside.

Add 1 skein of unmordanted wool yarn to the dye pot. Simmer for 1 hour, or until the yarn turns maroonish-red. Remove from dye bath.

Add a second skein of unmordanted wool yarn to the dye pot. Simmer for 1 hour, and then remove the dye pot from the heat and let the yarn steep overnight in the dye bath to absorb the remaining green and red colors, resulting in a brown color. Remove the yarn from the dye bath and set aside.

Reheat the dye bath to a simmer, and add the 1 remaining skein of alum-premordanted yarn. Simmer until the yarn turns yellow or gold, about 15 minutes.

Wash each skein separately with a pH-neutral soap, rinse thoroughly, and hang to dry.

This wild silk throw was dyed with St John's wort.

Elderberry

Elderberry (*Sambucus nigra*) is a wild, deciduous shrub or small tree found throughout Europe and North America. In the spring, the elder, or elderberry, tree has sprays of white flowers that develop into clumps of dark purple to black berries in the late summer. The leaves, bark, and berries of the plant create shades from blue to lavender and purple. You can make wine from elderberries, and the fruit has long been used for herbal remedies. You can even fry the flower sprays in batter as fritters. You can collect elderberries from the tree in the fall, if you have one in your yard or neighborhood, or you can obtain dried elderberries from herbal stores.

Try This:

Dye organic wool yarn with elderberries for an airy hand-knitted scarf.

ELDERBERRY-DYED WOOL KNIT SCARF

Knitting your own elderberry-dyed wool scarf can bring you relaxation during those long winter evenings, and the cozy scarf can be a comfort against the cold. A hand dyed and knitted scarf also makes a very special gift.

I knit my scarf with local organic wool, using chunky needles and a straight knit stitch for an open, airy effect. This dye recipe uses the berries of the elderberry tree, to dye the yarn before you knit the scarf. (Detailed information on dyeing wool yarn skeins follows.) Elderberries on wool yarn create a beautiful dusky gray-blue with an alum premordant. Premordant the wool yarn with alum before dyeing it (see Basic Alum Mordant with Wool, pages 40–41). If you want to work with a plant fiber, use Alum Mordant with Tannin-Treated Plant Fiber (page 47), and let the fiber soak in the dye solution for 1 to 2 days.

4 ounces (113 g) premordanted wool yarn skein
4 ounces (113 g) elderberries

Soak the premordanted wool yarn in water for at least
1 hour.

Crush the elderberries with a mortar and pestle.

Put the elderberries in a dye pot and cover with enough
water to cover the yarn. Bring the water to a simmer, 180°F
(82°C), and simmer for 1 hour. Turn off the heat, and let the
dye bath cool. Strain the plant parts from the water.

Add the premordanted, wetted wool yarn, and bring
the dye bath back up to a simmer. Simmer the wool yarn in
the dye liquid for 1 hour. Turn off the heat, and let the yarn
steep in the dye overnight.

Wash the yarn with pH-neutral soap, rinse thoroughly,
and hang to dry.

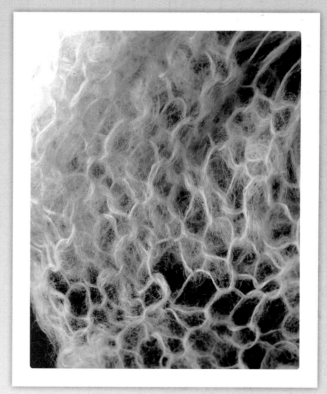

A hand-knitted wool scarf dyed with elderberry
makes the perfect winter gift.

Dyeing yarns can be an easy and rewarding way of working with natural color. By using locally sourced organic wool such as angora, alpaca wool, or sheep wool, you can achieve beautiful natural colors and be proud of supporting regional and sustainable agriculture. When dyeing yarn for knitting, weaving, or crocheting, you can use any of the dye recipes in this book to achieve satisfying color. Be sure to purchase wool yarn that has been scoured, so it's clean and ready to dye.

Yarn is wound into skeins before dyeing, to get the fiber ready to soak in the dye bath. This skein is being made from a spool of natural wool purchased from a knitting store.

WINDING A YARN SKEIN

If the yarn you purchased came in a spool or in a ball, you need to unwind it and make sure it is formed into a skein. When yarn is gathered in a skein, in the dye pot the color can move freely and evenly among the fibers to achieve even color saturation. The skein will also keep the yarn from tangling or matting while you're working. When winding your yarn into a skein for dyeing, create a skein that weighs no more than 8 ounces (227 g), so you can work with it easily in the dye pot.

Skeins are easy to make and don't require any special equipment or tools. You make a skein by winding the yarn in a circle. An easy way to do this is to wrap the yarn around the top of a chair back. You can also have someone hold their hands straight out in front, and you can wrap the yarn around them. Or you can sit and put your knees about a foot apart, and wrap the yarn around your knees. When you have wound about 8 ounces of yarn, tie off the ends, and put little ties around the skein at four equidistant spots, to keep the skein from coming unwound in the dye pot. Tie your skein tightly enough so your fibers won't come undone but loosely enough so the dye can flow evenly through the fibers. Lift the skein off the chair back or your friend's outstretched arms. It's ready to dye.

Handspun wool skeins hanging outside before dyeing.

DYEING WOOL YARN

Wool yarn can be dyed simply with plant color, or you can enhance the range of color results by using a mordant, a premordant, or an aftermordant. This technique uses a premordant and then proceeds to the dye process (see Basic Alum Mordant with Wool, pages 40–41, or Iron Aftermordant or Modifier, page 43). If you wish to use a premordant on the yarn and then store it for later dyeing projects, after the premordanting process you can wash, rinse, dry, label, and store it.

4 ounces (113g) wool yarn skein
1 recipe dye bath of your choice

Soak the skein of wool yarn in lukewarm water for at least 1 hour and preferably overnight to assure that the wool soaks up enough water to allow the mordant and the dye to effectively bond on the fiber.

Prepare a premordant bath for the wool yarn with alum or iron, and process the yarn skein. Premordanting the fiber assures that the mordant has properly bonded to the fiber before you place it in the plant dye bath, so you'll get optimal color results. You can also work with an iron after mordant as a modifier. The mordant will bond to the fiber usually within 10 to 15 minutes, depending on the color change you desire. You can also leave the fiber overnight for more saturated color.

After premordanting the wool yarn, wash the yarn with pH-neutral soap, rinse thoroughly, and hang to dry.

Prepare a dye bath with a dye recipe of your choice in this book. Strain all plant material and sediment from the dye bath. Plant material can be very difficult to remove from wool fiber. Let the dye cool down to lukewarm.

Place the premordanted, wetted yarn into the lukewarm dye bath, and place the dye pot on the stove. Gradually raise the temperature of water to a simmer, 180°F (82°C). Allow the yarn to gently simmer for 20 to 30 minutes, occasionally stirring gently so that the dye bath flows evenly among the fibers. Turn off the heat. Remove the yarn from the dye pot, or let the yarn steep in the dye bath overnight for more saturated color.

Wash the dyed yarn with pH-neutral soap in water of the same temperature as the cooled dye bath. Rinse the yarn thoroughly in the water of the same temperature as the wash water. Hang your dyed yarn skein to dry.

Your dyed yarn is now ready for any creative project.

Try This:
Create surprising hues for wool yarn with sour grass or red cabbage.

SOUR GRASS OR RED CABBAGE WOOL YARN

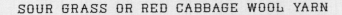

You can dye your wool yarns many different hues and shades, depending on whether a mordant is used, and which one. The wool yarns in the photo at top right were dyed with sour grass and different mordants. The colors in the photo bottom right were created by using red cabbage with and without different mordants.

ABOVE: *These luscious colors were made from sour grass, a sidewalk weed. The skeins were dyed (from left to right) with sour grass and no mordant, sour grass with an alum mordant, sour grass with an iron aftermordant and left overnight in the dye bath, and sour grass premordanted with alum and then mordanted with iron.* **CENTER:** *These yarns were dyed with red cabbage (left) and sour grass (right) and treated with different mordants.* **BELOW:** *These skeins of wool yarn were dyed with organic red cabbage from my local farmers market: (left to right) red cabbage with no mordant, red cabbage with an alum mordant, red cabbage with an iron mordant, and red cabbage with alum and iron mordants.*

PURCHASING NATURAL DYE MATERIALS

Many traditional dye plants that are long-standing botanical dye staples are available packaged or from a natural dye supply source. Again, just because the plant is considered "natural" does not necessarily mean that it is sustainable or good for you, even if it has been used as a natural dye source for a long time.

Logwood (*Haematoxylum campechianum*), a flowering tree from Mexico and Central America, is an example of an imported natural dye material associated with a heavy global carbon footprint. Logwood and also brazilwood (*Caesalpinia echinata*) are well-known traditional natural dye sources that produce bright colors in wool, cotton, and silk; logwood creates purples and brazilwood yields rich reds. The dyes are made from the heartwood of medium to large old-growth trees originally found in tropical forests, and are available commercially worldwide. But harvesting these old-growth trees can be devastating to their ecosystem.

If purchasing dried dye plant materials, make sure that the products come from a certified organic, fair trade, sustainable source. See Resources, beginning on page 154.

Chapter 4

A Plant Palette

Sample Plants and Dye Colors

Nature is a phenomenal color library. There is no better way to be inspired by color than to notice the natural world. Looking closely at botanical color is one of the best ways of creating an interesting plant palette to work with. Noticing the depth of burgundy, pink, and green in the tip of a cherry leaf, the rich brown shades in healthy soil, or the deep blue of lake water on a sunny day can all be inspirations for your color experiments.

Naturally dyed textile swatches reveal a range of brilliant colors.

OPPOSITE PAGE, ABOVE LEFT: *A daylily bud in the garden creates a striking silhouette against a white wall, a reminder that inspiration is everywhere.* **OPPOSITE PAGE, BELOW LEFT:** *These naturally dyed, colorful wools are ready for knitting projects.* **OPPOSITE PAGE, RIGHT:** *These beautiful yarns were dyed from botanical materials destined for the compost pile, by my students at California College of the Arts.*

INSPIRATION IN NATURE

It is a great exercise to take a walk, whether in your neighborhood or in your garden, and to choose three striking leaves, sticks, or stones that blow you away with their color palette. Just simply picking up a natural object from your garden and spending just a moment to notice what you see allows the expansiveness of color to become more apparent and awe inspiring.

Recognizing the differences between hues found in nature, the light and dark shades, and variations in tones can be a great tool to help you in developing a natural dye color palette. Interior designers often comment that one of the best methods for designing a room is by choosing your colors based on a colorful leaf that appeals to you. The same can be done for your textiles. Inspiration is all around us. All we need is openness and the ability to feel it.

The plant materials listed here are just a few of the nontoxic and diverse wild dye plants you may be able to find in your local market or even grow in your garden from seed. Some of these plant materials can even be found in your kitchen cupboard. These botanical sources yield a wide palette of reliable, interesting dye colors. You can use simple methods to extract the dye from these plant materials, whether applying

heat on a burner, employing solar dyeing, doing sun tea dyeing, or soaking in cold water.

In addition to these wild plant dyes, the Natural Dye Color Chart shows you the actual hues and shades you can achieve from a selection of dye plants.

With natural dyes, it's important to understand color and what happens when you mix colors. Red, yellow, and blue are primary colors, and cannot be created from two different sources. You can mix two primary color sources to get secondary colors: for example blue and yellow make green, blue and red make purple, red and yellow make orange. By mixing secondary colors, you get colors that represent a combination of those two hues: for example, green and purple will create a brown. Black, brown, and gray can be created by mixing several colors together. But these results can vary and depend on the chemical compatibility of the dyes you are working with.

LEFT: *Both the leaves and berries of the ivy plant produce dye color. The berries are a favored food for birds but toxic to humans and should only be used by experts for dyeing.* **CENTER:** *Natural fibers can be dyed in a broad range of botanical colors.* **RIGHT:** *Finding intriguing colors in nature can be as simple as looking around you. Lichen growing on an old apple tree offers the contrast of a mossy gray-green against a dark rich brown.*

Sources for Natural Dye Colors

Yellows

CALENDULA (*Calendula officinalis*) FLOWERS

CHAMOMILE (*Anthemis tinctoria*) FLOWERS

DAHLIA (*Dahlia* species) FLOWERS

GOLDENROD (*Solidago canadensis*) FLOWERS

MARIGOLD (*Tagetes* species) FLOWERS

QUEEN ANNE'S LACE (*Daucus carota*) FLOWERS

TANSY FLOWERS (*Tanacetum vulgare*) FLOWERS

WELD (*Reseda luteola*) PLANT PARTS

CATNIP (*Nepeta cataria*) PLANT PARTS

Greens

ARTICHOKE (*Cynara cardunculus*) PLANT PARTS

BLACK-EYED SUSAN (*Rudbeckia hirta*) FLOWERS, LEAVES, STEMS

HYSSOP (*Hyssopus* species) PLANT PARTS

IVY (*Hedera helix*) LEAVES

PLANTAIN (*Musa ×paradisiaca*) PLANT PARTS

Pinks

AMARANTH (*Amaranthus retroflexus*) FLOWERS

BIRCH (*Betula* species) BARK

SORREL (*Rumex acetosa*) ROOT

Reds

DANDELION (*Taraxacum officinale*) ROOT

LADY'S BEDSTRAW (*Galium verum*) ROOT

SPRUCE (*Picea abies*) CONES

Blue-Purples

CORNFLOWER (*Centaurea cyanus*) FLOWERS

INDIGO (*Indigofera tinctoria*) LEAVES

GRAPE (*Vitis* species) SKINS

Browns

COMFREY (*Symphytum officinale*) LEAVES

LARCH (*Larix pinaceae*) NEEDLES

WILD AMERICAN PLUM (*Prunus americana*) ROOT

Grays and Blacks

ALDER (*Alnus* species) BARK

IRIS (*Iris douglasiana*) ROOT

POPLAR (*Populus* species) LEAVES

NATURAL DYE COLOR CHART

This color chart will help you to choose a plant color that suits your dye project. You will find recipes for many of these colors in this book. For each plant, four dye color swatches are shown according to the mordant used:

1. *no mordant*
2. *an alum mordant*
3. *an iron mordant*
4. *an alum mordant and an iron mordant*

(The one exception to this sequence of mordants in the chart is noted for St John's wort flowers, which have special characteristics as a dye.)

The swatches give you a sense of the range of gorgeous colors you can create with different dyeing processes. You can find more discussion of these plant materials, how to process them, the dyes they yield, and the dye recipes in this book (see the index). There are always variations in the natural dye process, so just use these colors as a general guide, and record the results of your dye experiments, including the water pH and the freshness of the plant material, for optimal accuracy in repeating your results.

ACORN • Acorns can be collected under oak trees in the fall, or you can buy acorn powder. Soak ground acorns in water for several days to get the full color intensity. Acorns create colors from light beiges to dark grays and teal blues.

BLACKBERRY LEAVES • Blackberry leaves can be just as valuable for dyes as the berries. Blackberry leaves create tones from yellow-greens to deep teals and dark grays.

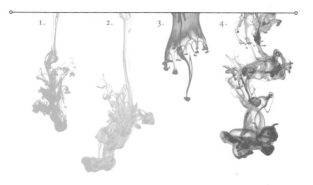

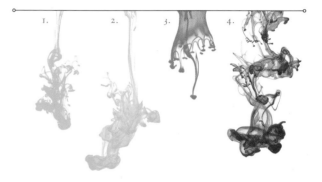

BLACKBERRY FRUIT • Blackberries are not only delicious but can be used for interesting color projects. Blackberry bushes are abundant in many regions in North America. Forage for blackberries in early fall. Blackberries create shades from light lavenders to blue-grays.

BLACK WALNUT HULL • Black walnuts can be gathered in season. Hull the nuts, and crush the hulls. Or black walnut hull can be obtained in powdered form at specialist herbal and grocery stores. Black walnut hull creates many shades of warm, dark brown.

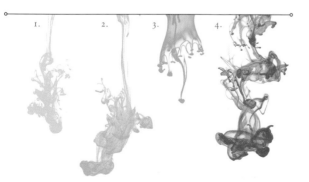

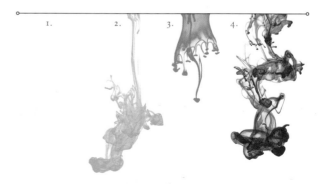

ELDERBERRY • The fruit of the elderberry tree has traditionally been used as a cure for sore throats. The berries can also make beautiful colors in the dye bath. Elderberries produce light to dark shades of purples and blue-grays, depending on the mordant used.

FIG LEAVES • Growing a fig tree in your yard can be great for both dye experiments and delicious meals. Fig leaves make an excellent dye source for yellows and greens.

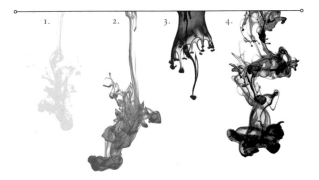

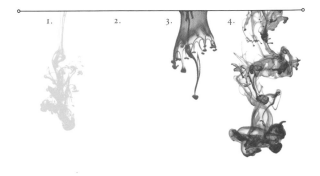

FENNEL • Fennel is a tall herbaceous plant that can be foraged in vacant lots and can be grown in your garden. Fennel flowers and plant parts create bright yellows and deep greens, depending on the mordant used.

JAPANESE MAPLE LEAVES • Japanese maple leaves are an antiseptic and can smell much like hibiscus tea in the dye pot. The leaves of red Japanese maple create natural dye colors of light pink to stormy blue-grays.

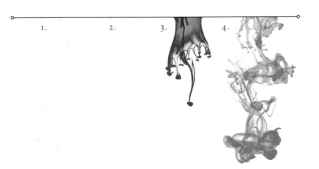

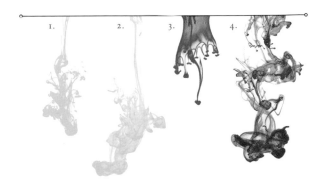

LAVENDER • Lavender is not only a natural insect repellant for your fibers; it is also a dye for beautiful, subtle tones. Lavender yields colors from beige-yellow to light lavender to dusky-gray, depending on the mordant used.

MADDER ROOT • Madder can be fun to grow from seed, and creates rewarding vibrant colors. Madder root is ground up for use as a dye source, and can be found at most specialty dye and textile suppliers. Madder root creates oranges to deep rich reds.

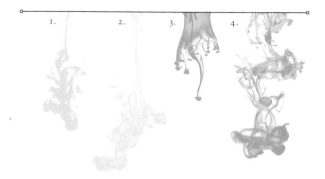

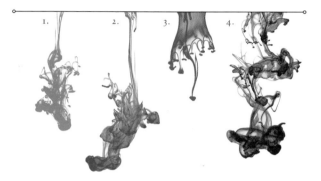

MINT LEAVES • You can grow mint easily in the garden. It smells wonderful in the dye bath. Mint leaves make dye colors of mint-greens and grays.

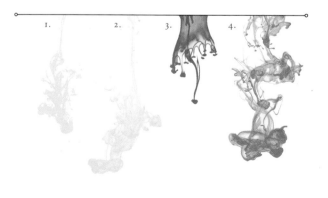

OLIVE FRUIT • Ripe black olives fresh from the tree provide a rich color source for dye. Black olive fruit can create gorgeous pinks to teals.

ONIONSKINS • Onionskins are the gift that keeps on giving. After you peel onions when cooking and before you throw the onionskins onto your compost pile, use them to create gorgeous dyes of rusty oranges, golds, and deep greens.

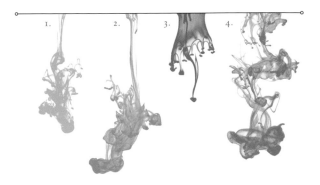

OLIVE LEAVES • The leaves from pruned olive branches can be used to turn green waste into colorful natural dyes from light yellows to deep gray-greens.

RED CABBAGE • Cabbage is a wonderful dye to experiment with, since it is so readily available in your local farmers market and is easy to grow. Red cabbage leaves can make beautiful blues, lavenders, and silver-grays.

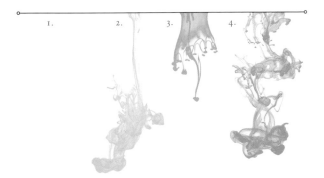

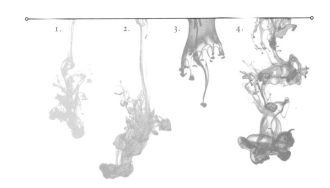

SOUR GRASS FLOWERS & PLANT PARTS
Sour grass (Bermuda buttercup) is a common springtime weed, and creates striking colors with or without heat on both animal and plant fibers. You can get the brightest yellow-green dye with the flowers, but the leaves and the flowers together also create a similar color.

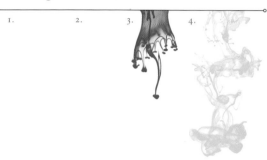

TURMERIC ROOT • Turmeric root can be obtained in powdered form at your local grocery store. If you live in a tropical climate, you can grow turmeric and make a homegrown dye. Ground turmeric root yields yellows and deep greens.

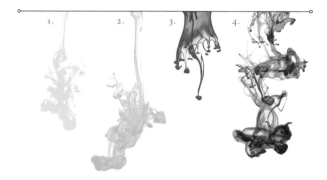

ST JOHN'S WORT FLOWERS • St John's wort has traditionally been used as nature's mood booster, but it can also create some beautiful happy colors. This dye plant can be coaxed to create many hues, from yellows to greens.

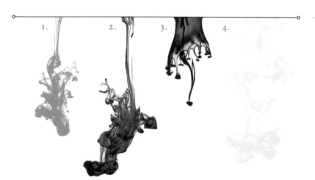

{ FOR ST JOHN'S WORT SWATCHES ONLY }

1. *alum*

2. *no mordant*

3. *no mordant*

4. *alum*

Chapter 5

The Joy of Slow Textiles

The Simple Pleasures
of Making Your World More Colorful

Cultivating color deeply satisfies your creative urges, whether it is through growing your own dye garden, making a tasty colorful meal, pruning vivid plants in your garden, or using weeds to create wondrous dye hues. Taking the time to connect with each step in the process and then relishing the results can be endlessly rewarding.

Planting a garden can be easy, whether you choose vegetables, herbs, or more traditional dye plants.

THE SLOW MOVEMENT

*Dye plants can be grown anywhere, in a window box
or in pots on a sunny windowsill.*

The Slow Movement began in the 1990s as an international protest against the speed of modern culture's processes, which had accelerated in many forms since the Industrial Revolution. The movement was initiated by the Slow Food movement, which is opposed to a culture of fast food and fast life, and dedicated to encouraging a renewed appreciation of the food we eat, where it comes from, how it tastes, and how our food choices affect the rest of the world. Slow Food brings together pleasure and responsibility and makes them inseparable.

The Slow Movement has expanded in many directions, including Slow Art, Slow Travel, and Slow Parenting, with a general principle of everyone's participating in life's experiences at his or her own speed and finding enjoyment in connecting with and preserving traditional life ways. The "slowness" doesn't refer to the length of time involved in making or doing something. It points instead to an expanded state of awareness in our every daily activity, and the potential for a richer range of experience for individuals and communities.

I have been greatly inspired by the sustainable food movement in California. There is an investment in quality that comes through the slow approach. The quality, innovation, and application of creating a textile yourself, supporting or appreciating a textile or garment from a community or artisan that practices slow and sustainable techniques, or taking the time to trace the life cycle of a garment or textiles from another area of the world are all very much connected to the Slow Movement.

Food led the way in the modern sustainability revolution, and clothing and shelter came next. We don't literally consume clothing or textiles, but the production of textiles uses the same resources that are required to make food: land, water, air, and soil. Questions of biodiversity and healthy production apply equally to both. Like food, clothing is not just a basic need, but a mode of personal and cultural expression. Values of the Slow Movement are care and consideration for where materials come from and those who make them, support of long-lasting quality goods, and general environ-

LEFT: *Lichen found fallen on the forest floor was used to color this textile.* **RIGHT:** *Lichen should never be picked off trees, but only collected from fallen branches. Some lichens take up to 100 years to grow, and they are an important part of the ecosystem.*

mental stewardship. From Slow Food to Slow Fashion and Slow Textiles, a culture is being reborn of connection to community, ecoliteracy, and a personal sense of place.

Authentic understanding of and connection to where our materials derive from can lead to building diversity and supporting sustainability in broad ways. As you draw upon the vast range of natural fibers and dyes, you are supporting biodiversity in the sources of your fibers and dyes. Learning more about the fibers and dyes of your own bioregion will also in turn build biodiversity. Supporting a wide range of natural fiber and dye sources, rather than purchasing monocropped plant material, can be your contribution toward creating a more diversified agriculture and vibrant culture. Sustainability is dependent on biodiversity, care of a clean and healthy land, and a vibrant culture. A greater effect of encouraging and supporting biodiversity can be species diversity and species richness.

No matter what kind of textile work you are interested in—whether designing, weaving, sewing, knitting, felting, or others—creating and dyeing your own textiles from organic materials is profoundly fulfilling. When you make your own textiles and dyes, you are reaching back into a long history of the handmade and bringing it into the everyday, which will give you a satisfying relationship with the creative process and will stimulate originality in your work.

The slow approach has the ability to tell a story, to weave worlds and to welcome wonder into the common experience of daily existence. Creating what you need with your own hands and supporting others who are doing the same in their own individual ways builds both culture and diversity. Slow Textiles are defined by our ability to appreciate the origins and qualities of materials and to think through the design and the entire creation process from seed to seed—growing your plant from seed, harvesting it, and gathering the seed to be sown again—or from garden to garment. It is an efficient and satisfying process.

MAKING SLOW TEXTILES

As you delve further into the realm of natural dyes, you will find endless interesting projects where you will be able to work with both fiber and dyes from scratch. When making something with your own hands, you have the chance to reflect on modern culture, which typically relies on store-bought, mass-produced textiles.

As a consumer, understanding how both industrially produced and artisan-created textiles are made and where they come from are important steps toward knowing how to support more sustainable practices for both people and the environment.

Using Organic Fibers and Dyes

Using organic fibers and dyes and supporting organizations that produce these materials are better for the ecosystem and all nature's creatures. Using these clean materials leads to a healthier planet.

Choosing to purchase organic raw wool can be a way of supporting your local vendors at the farmers markets in your community and supporting the organic agriculture of your region. Raw wool is the freshly harvested fleece that has not yet been scoured or spun. Finding and dyeing local organic wool is an easy, enticing way for you to begin to create slow and sustainable textiles.

Sheep wool comes in many beautiful shades beyond white. You can experiment with dyeing wool that is gray, brown, gold, or another natural shade, and in the process you can learn a lot about overdyeing, or dyeing fiber that already has a base color. Overdyeing brown wool with madder root as your dye source, for example, will create a rich, deep brownish-red. Overdyeing brown wool with a yellow dye source will create ochre.

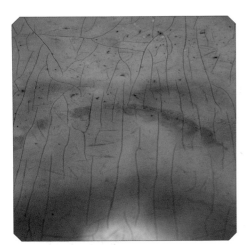  

LEFT: *The whole process of natural dyeing can be a beautiful activity, including watching nontoxic color after it is finished in the dye pot.* **CENTER:** *Dyeing different fabrics with one cabbage dye bath can result in many different color tones.* **RIGHT:** *A natural dye bath reflects the garden setting.*

  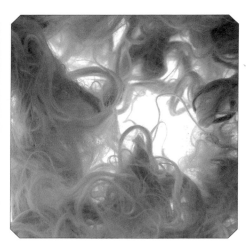

LEFT: *Watching trees like this star magnolia change through the seasons is a way to know and appreciate your environment.* **CENTER:** *This naturally dyed blanket was created by one of my textile students. What you choose to make with your naturally dyed fibers is an exciting realm to explore.* **RIGHT:** *I purchased this alpaca fiber from a local farmer. Going to the source for your fibers can be as rewarding as going to the source for your dyes.*

Felting

Wool felt, a good example of a Slow Textile, is one of the world's oldest textiles. Felt samples have been found in archeological sites dating back to at least 6500 BCE. Wool felt has been a staple in traditional clothing and architecture. Felted wool traditionally was used in central Asia to make yurts warm, durable, and lightweight. Felt has a rich cultural history, with many slow traditions and stories that support the craft. Creating a simple felt project can be exciting and inspiring.

Felt is created by layering wet wool fiber and adding friction to the layers in a continuing process so that the fibers stitch to each other, and applying water—boiling hot, then cold, then hot—which shrinks and mats the fibers. If you examine wool fibers under a microscope, you'll see that they contain small scales, and when you work them against each other, they will interweave. Felted wool can be as thin or as thick as the number of layers you use. Felt is smooth and soft, and is easy to care for: it can be hand-washed and air-dried.

Gather enough raw wool fiber for the project you would like to complete. Keep in mind that your felt will shrink once it becomes felted—approximately 30 percent—so plan your project accordingly.

Before dyeing the wool, you will need to both scour the raw wool (see Preparing Animal Fibers for Dyeing, page 29) and card it. Carding is a process of combing the wool with two carding combs, which look like brushes, to break up the natural fiber clumps, shed plant bits, and align the fibers so they can be easily worked with. Carding wool is also an easy way to blend different kinds and colors of fiber into a homogeneous substance. Carding combs are easy to use. You can get carding combs and instructions for using them at weaving and spinning shops or on the Internet. Wool batting that is already scoured and carded for spinning or felting can be bought from specialty textile suppliers and knitting shops, and often can be found at farmers markets.

Try This:
Make your own laptop case by felting and
dyeing the wool [no sewing involved].

MINT-DYED FELTED LAPTOP CASE

Making your own felted laptop case is an easy way to
create a useful, stylish, and protective cover for your
personal computer. You can dye the wool fleece and use
it to create different items, or you can felt a wool item
and dye it afterward, like the mint dip-dyed laptop case
featured in this project. Your felted computer case does
not need any sewing, since hand-felting allows you to
easily create seamless shapes. Measure your laptop, and
make your wool layers twice as deep as your computer
(the layers will be folded over) and a bit more than 30
percent larger in depth and width, to allow for shrinkage.
For this project you will need Mint Dye (page 119) and
Iron Aftermordant or Modifier (page 43).

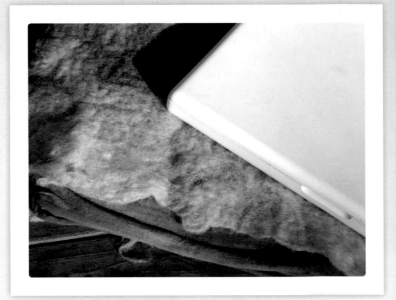

Keep your laptop in "mint" condition with a felted computer case.

Carded and scoured wool ready for felting

Old plastic water bottle with a squirt top or holes punched through the cap.

pH-neutral soap, ½ teaspoon per 1 pint (237 ml) water

Boiling water source, like a teakettle

Recycled bubble wrap (with tiny bubbles), long enough to be twice as wide as your felt piece is at first

Heavy cardboard packing tube longer than your project will be wide

Towel for soaking up excess water

Create 4 layers of carded wool. Build the first layer so that all the fibers are laid in one direction, then build a second layer on top of the first with fibers running perpendicular to the fibers in the first layer. Repeat, to build a third layer and a four layer. Your layers will be approximately 1 ½ to 2 inches (3.8 to 5.1 cm) high, and will shrink to about ¼ to ½ inch (0.6 to 1.3 cm) high. (If you want a thicker felted piece, you can pile up more layers.) Having the layers stacked like cake layers will allow the fibers to interlock.

Fill an old squirt-top water bottle with hot water and add the soap. Pour the hot, soapy water over the four layers of wool fiber until they are saturated.

Lay the bubble wrap on your worktable, place the stack of wool layers on it, and fold the bubble wrap over the pile of wool fiber, enclosing the pile. Roll the bubble-wrap–felt layers around the cardboard tube. Roll the tube back and forth on the worktable, applying even pressure. At intervals, stop and unroll the bubble-wrapped wool, to check on the felt, adding hot soapy water to help the fibers lock to each other. Then resume rolling the tube back and forth, right to left, left to right, stopping every so often to change directions. The wool layers will start to felt after approximately 20 minutes.

When your felt is beginning to form but it is not so tightly felted that you can't pick the fibers apart, lift the bubble wrap off the top, fold the felt piece over on itself, and apply friction and hot soapy water to both sides of the felt, rubbing the felt vigorously with your palms against the bubble wrap. As the case sides start to felt together, continue to use your hands to create friction in any spot that needs more binding, alternating hand rubbing and hot soapy water, for 30 to 45 minutes.

When the case is felted solidly at the seams, creating a pocket for the computer to slide in, it's finished. Rinse thoroughly in lukewarm water, and lay flat to dry.

To dye the felted laptop case, soak the felted case in water for at least 1 hour.

Prepare the mint dye.

Add an iron modifier.

After the dye and the iron modifier are mixed and the dye bath is a dark green-gray color, remove it from the heat and cool to room temperature.

Carefully dip the bottom of your wetted, felted case into the dye bath. Clip the case to the side of the pot with clothespins, and allow the case bottom to absorb the dye for 20 to 30 minutes or overnight if you want a darker color.

Remove the case from the dye, wash with pH-neutral soap in lukewarm water, rinse until the water runs clear, and lay flat to dry.

COLOR AND COMMUNITY

Slow Textiles are as much about community and culture as they are about the creative process and results. There are many ways to be involved with the Slow Movement, whether it is through Slow Cities, Slow Food, or Slow Textiles.

A community garden is an invaluable place to work and make connection with the web of life. In the garden there is balance. It becomes an equalizer as humans and nature work together for the same principles that allow each to thrive. Connecting with a local school or community garden and volunteering time in the garden tending, growing dye and fiber plants, or using plant waste as color sources, can be inspiring. It is a wonderful way to teach ecology and material culture, while bringing art back into education. Working with natural color, students are often awestruck by the potential that a plant possesses and eager to share their newfound discoveries with their classmates, friends, and family.

Storytelling, recipes, and making colors from scratch are a good way to get people into the garden. Much of what I love about natural dyes is telling the story of where the color comes from, what connects us to the particular place, plant, and culture. There is much to be uncovered in natural dyeing, and a great way of enjoying the process is sharing information with each other, starting natural dyeing groups, supporting gardens, and communicating with your neighbors to see if they have waste products for your color projects.

Using truly sustainable processes is not only about working with materials; it can also be about assuring that future generations will enjoy the process as well. Working with younger (and older) ages can be a great way of sharing knowledge and getting the most out of your dye bath—both with the materials and with the sense of community it creates.

LEFT: *Heirloom plants grown in healthy soil thrive in my organic plant dye garden.* **RIGHT:** *Teaching classes about nontoxic, colorful plant dyes can be a great way to volunteer at your local community garden.*

HEIRLOOM PLANTS AND DYES

Heirloom plants are plants that were commonly grown throughout history. Before the industrialization of agriculture, humans grew a wider variety of plants and vegetables for food and other plant by-products. In recent years, a return to growing heirloom plants has become for some a reaction against agribusiness and monocropping, or growing the same crop year after year on the same land without crop rotation.

Heirloom plants have many beneficial characteristics. They are often genetically resilient to local pests, diseases, and extreme weather, making them ecologically sound plants to work with in your garden for a hardy harvest. Bees and other insects will naturally pollinate heirloom plants, so by growing and using these plants, you contribute to natural biodiversity. And by gathering and sharing the seeds of your heirloom plants—your brightest colored hollyhocks, your tastiest onions, or your plants that withstood the driest summers or the coldest winters—you are ensuring future existence of these strong plants. Sharing heirloom seeds is a rewarding activity and has been gaining much popularity in North America and Europe over the past decade.

The variety of heirloom plants provides interesting tastes, garden design elements, and dye color shades. Many people grow heirloom varietals to learn how to grow historical plants, while others are looking toward the future and thinking about ensuring genetic diversity. Nonprofit organizations, like Seed Savers Exchange, support gardeners in sharing and passing on both knowledge of how to find heirloom seeds and how to grow them.

Madder Root

If you research heirloom plants, you will discover that there are many interesting varietals to work with that yield unusual natural dye colors. Madder root, for instance, is an ancient primary dye plant that creates a rare, true plant-based rich red that is difficult to find. Madder root is fun to grow in your garden. It can take up to 2 years to harvest the root, but the red color it yields is worth it, and it is easy to dye with. Common madder (*Rubia tinctorum*) can grow to 5 feet (1.5 m) in height. The roots, which can be over 3 feet (1 m) long, are the source of the dye.

Saved and shared seeds are truly the gifts that keep on giving.

{ RECIPE }

MADDER ROOT DYE

Madder root creates rich vibrant red, oranges, and pinks. You can get these colors without using a mordant, as in this recipe, but you can also get rich colors through mordanting with alum, mordanting with iron, and mordanting with alum and then an iron modifier (see the Natural Dye Color Chart, beginning on page 132). You can create more orange shades without a mordant, and more true reds with premordanting with alum. Prepare three batches of fiber or several projects to dye (like wool gloves and wool yarn), to get the most out of your madder dye bath before the color is exhausted. Madder works on both animal and plant fibers—richness of color will depend on length of time in the dye bath and mordants chosen. You can process your own homegrown madder root, or you can purchase ground madder root from natural dye and textile suppliers.

4 ounces (113 g) fiber
4 ounces (113 g) madder root

TOP: *Fabric dyed from madder root by a student at the California College of the Arts.* **CENTER:** *Madder root will yield scarlet reds, oranges, and burnt ambers in the dye pot.* **BOTTOM:** *An angora wool sweater soaking in a madder root dye bath.*

Soak the fiber in water for at least 1 hour.

Soak the madder root for several days to soften it. Then use a mortar and pestle to grind it, or grind it in an old blender that you just use for dye projects.

Add the ground madder to a dye pot full of water, and slowly heat to the simmering point, 180°F (82°C). Simmer for 40 minutes. Turn off the heat, and let the madder steep overnight for rich red shades.

Add your wetted unmordanted fiber to the dye bath, and bring the dye bath to a simmer. Simmer for 20 to 40 minutes. It will be a rich red-salmon color. Remove the fiber from the dye bath and set aside.

Add a second batch of wetted fiber to the same dye bath, to get a lighter shade of red-pink. Remove and set aside.

Add a third batch of wetted fiber to the same dye bath, to get peachy colors.

MADDER GLOVES

Luxurious fingerless gloves made from an old cashmere sweater were dyed with madder root without the use of a mordant.

MADDER YARN

Wool yarn dyed with madder root and premordanted with alum can create this wonderful shade of red. Adding a second batch of yarn to the same dye bath would yield a lighter shade.

SEEDS TO SEW

You will gain a wealth of knowledge by growing your own dye plants "from soil to studio."
The process allows you to fully experience the joy of making Slow Textiles from the very beginning
and to savor the meaning of knowing exactly where your color comes from.

Natural color bursting with beauty, in and out of the dye pot.

One of my most influential experiences with botanical color came from a workshop I took in my mid-twenties at the Darthia Farm in the region of Maine where I lived as a child. The workshop was a strong reminder that much of the knowledge I had been seeking around the globe about sustainable textiles was practiced in America in the hands of women who were also farmers. The workshop also confirmed the power that comes with community sharing of natural dye recipes, other hands-on knowledge, and seed saving exchanges.

Organic farmers and fiber artists led the workshop on the ancient dye plants that yield primary colors: indigo, madder, and weld. These women had been growing these plants and sharing the seeds and starter plants. I was so moved by the seed exchange at the end of the workshop that it inspired me to end natural dye classes I teach with a seed exchange of dye and fiber plants. It also inspired me to create a program called Seeds to Sew through the Permacouture Institute.

Seed saving is an essential way of sharing the source of your color materials. Many people gather for seed-saving swaps around the world, supporting both biodiversity and community in the process.

How to Save Seeds

Saving seeds contributes to sustainability. Many plants will adapt to local bioregions and be uniquely pollinated, making the seed a part of the local history as well. Some seed-saving tips are:

☐ The best time to harvest seeds is when the plant is at its most ripe or mature. This time is usually autumn for most summer-flowering plants.

☐ Collecting seeds from your dye plants can be easy. Collect seeds in a paper bag. Store saved seeds in sealed envelopes in an airtight box in a cool dark place (like a fridge), until you are ready to plant them. Planting the seeds at the beginning of the next season assures best results from your saved seeds.

☐ Some seeds are protected by lots of fleshy tissue, and some are held within capsules. Collect those seeds when the pods or capsules turn brown.

☐ Some seeds may be sticky and need cleaning before they are stored—for example, pumpkin and squash seeds. Wash those seeds and spread them out on a towel to dry, before you store them.

☐ Tag the seeds so that you'll know what they are when it's time to plant.

Working from seed to seed can give you the ultimate feeling of a successful harvest. Saving your seeds and using the color from the plants that your grow supports self-sufficiency and helps the color to keep on giving. This is truly regenerative design.

Growing your own dye plants can also bring friends and community together. Hosting seed-saving swaps is a great way to multiply the variety in your garden without spending more than the cost of a package of seed. Many botanical gardens, community gardens, and other public entities may also have seed-saving swaps or may be a good place to start something.

Keeping the tradition and knowledge of natural dyeing alive preserves a wealth of cultural, environmental, and practical information that will encourage biodiversity for generations to come.

Cultivating color can bring a lifetime of inspiration.

ACID: a chemical that will produce a pH of less than 7 in a water solution.

ALKALI: a chemical that will produce a pH of greater than 7 in a water solution. Alkali is essentially the opposite of an acid. The most common alkalis used in dyeing include sodium carbonate (soda ash) and sodium bicarbonate (baking soda).

ALUM MORDANT: nontoxic metallic compound used to help extract and modify dye color. Several compounds called alum are used as mordants, including aluminum potassium sulfate, or pickling alum, and aluminum sulfate, which is the alum most used in textile arts and also used in municipal water filtration.

BIOREGION: an ecologically and geographically defined area. Biodiversity of flora, fauna, and ecosystems of an area are usually defined by bioregions.

CARBON FOOTPRINT: a measure in units of carbon dioxide of the amount of greenhouse gases we emit directly or indirectly into the atmosphere by our daily actions.

CELLULOSE FIBER: plant fiber consisting of a structural polysaccharide made by plants. Units very similar to glucose are assembled into huge molecules that form strong fibers. Cellulose, or plant, textiles include cotton, jute, hemp, and linen.

DIRECT APPLICATION: a method by which a dye solution is applied to areas of fabric by techniques such as painting, squirting, spraying, and stamping.

DYE: in textile terms, a soluble colorant that attaches to fibers in molecular form.

ECOLITERACY: a term coined by environmentalist Fritjof Capra, meaning education for sustainable living. The reasoning behind ecoliteracy is that if we learn to understand our environment emotionally and deeply rather than through lecturing or abstract fact-based knowledge, we will be motivated to care for it.

ETHICAL FASHION: an approach to the design, sourcing, and manufacture of clothing that includes both social and environmental consciousness. Sustainable fashion—using environmentally friendly materials and methods in clothing production—is part of this movement.

FAIR TRADE: an organized social movement and market-based approach to alleviating global poverty and promoting sustainability. The movement promotes the payment of a fair price as well as social and environmental standards in all areas related to the production of goods.

FELTING: a method by which wool fibers interlock to create a textile.

IRON MORDANT: the use of iron sulfate or ferrous sulfate as a common mordant material to affect the color of natural dyes.

LIGHTFASTNESS: a measure of how resistant a dye material is to fading caused by exposure to light. Lightfastness mostly depends on the molecular structure of the dye itself, but can be influenced by the fiber or the presence of contaminants.

MORDANT: a chemical that aids attachment of a dyestuff to fibers by bonding to both the fiber and the dye, and affects the hue produced with certain dyestuffs. Mordants are necessary for dyes that have very low or no natural affinity for the fiber. Mordants can be applied before (premordant), with, or after (aftermordant) the dye, depending on the nature of the dye, the fiber, and the mordant.

NATURAL FIBER: a fiber obtained from a plant, animal, or mineral. The natural fibers may be classified by their origin as cellulose (from plants), protein (from animals), and mineral.

ORGANIC CLOTHING: clothing that is made from materials that are raised or grown without the use of chemicals in the form of pesticides and herbicides.

OVERDYE: to dye a naturally colored fiber, or to dye a fabric that has already been dyed.

PH: a measure of the concentration of hydronium in a solution. Acid solutions have a pH less than 7; alkaline solutions have a pH greater than 7. A pH of 7 is neutral. The normal pH range is 0 to 14.

PIGMENT: a colored substance that is insoluble in water, usually in the form of a fine powder. Pigments are used to color many types of paint, including some textile paints, and almost all inks used for silkscreen printing.

PROTEIN FIBER: biological polymers made up of amino acids. All hair-based fibers, like wool, mohair, and angora, are protein, or animal-based, fibers. Silk is also a protein fiber.

SCOUR: to thoroughly wash fiber or fabric to remove contaminants before the dyeing process.

SHIBORI: a Japanese tie-dyeing technique. In shibori, fabric is folded, twisted, tied, or wrapped, and then dyed. When unfolded, patterns emerge.

SIMMER: a very low boil, where bubbles emerge from the bottom of the pot but the water doesn't roll, 180°F (82°C).

STAINLESS STEEL: a broad class of corrosion-resistant metals. Stainless steel is often recommended for vessels for dyeing. It is made of iron alloyed with metals such as chromium, molybdenum, nickel, and others.

SUSTAINABILITY: a characteristic of a process or state that can be maintained at a consistent level indefinitely. A sustainable process meets the needs of the present without compromising the ability of future generations to meet their own needs.

TANNIC ACID: a mixture of compounds derived from oak bark, galls, acorns, and other natural sources. Tannic acid treatment is used to improve the washfastness of dyed fiber.

UPCYCLING: the reusing of a material to create an object of greater purpose.

WASHFASTNESS: a measure of the resistance of a dye to washing out of the fiber.

INFORMATION AND SUPPLIES

AUSTRALIA

Batik Oetoro: a textile supply resource for a range of natural dye supplies. *www.dyeman.com*.

Beautiful Silks: purveyor of silk and other natural textiles including wools, linens, and cottons for the textile artist. *www.beautifulsilks.com*.

Morning Star Crafts: good resource for natural dye supplies and mordants, and carded natural wool fleece. *www.morningstarcrafts.com.au*.

Seed Savers Australia: a great source for seed saving in Australia. *www.seedsavers.net*.

CANADA

Canadian Ecology Centre: a natural choice for experiential learning and living. *www.canadianecology.ca*.

Maiwa Textiles: good source of natural dyes, instruction, and workshops. *www.maiwa.com*.

Royal Botanical Gardens: Canada's largest botanical garden and an excellent resource for learning more about fiber and dye-producing plants. *www.rbg.ca*.

Seed and Plant Sanctuary for Canada: a charitable organization dedicated to the health and vitality of the earth through the preservation and promotion of heritage seeds. *www.seedsanctuary.com*.

Seeds of Diversity: Canadian volunteer organization that conserves the biodiversity and traditional knowledge of food crops and garden plants as well as a seed library. *www.seeds.ca*.

Slow Food Canada: regional resource for Slow Food International. *www.slowfood.ca*.

NEW ZEALAND

Blue House Yarns: a source for a beautiful array of naturally dyed organic wool yarns. *www.bluehouseyarns.co.nz*.

Hands: wool and natural dye supplies. *www.hands.co.nz*.

Organic Pathways: online New Zealand guide to organic living, including gardening classes, resources for organic seeds, and other useful tips. *www.organicpathways.co.nz*.

Seed Savers Resources: seed saving network resource for New Zealand. *www.seedsavers.org.nz*.

Treliske Organics: source for organic wool yarns. *www.treliskeorganic.com*.

Wheels and Whorls: everything for the felt lover in New Zealand. Wet felting, nuno felting, and needle felting supplies and kits. Felting wools: New Zealand merino, corriedale, and polwarth, available in dyed and natural colors. Wide range of related fiber supplies: wool carders, dyes, weaving looms, and spinning wheels. www.wheelsandshorls.co.nz.

UNITED KINGDOM

Avant-Gardening: Creative Organic Gardening. www.advantgardening.org.uk.

Annie Sherburne: ecological yarn and environmentally friendly textiles. www.anniesherburne.co.uk.

Ardalanish-Isle in Mull: Beautiful Tweeds from Native Breeds. www.ardalanishfarm.co.uk.

BBC Gardening: A great site for finding how-to videos, and a great blog with gardening advice. www.bbc.co.uk.

Center for Contemporary Art and the Natural World: "A culture is no better than its woods." —W. H. Auden. http://www.ccanw.co.uk.

Crafts Council. www.craftscouncil.org.uk.

Dyework: spinning and dyeing courses in London. www.dyework.co.uk.

Eco Textile News: online magazine for sustainable textiles and clothing. www.ecotextile.com.

Ethical Fashion Forum (EFF): not-for profit network focusing on social and environmental sustainability in the fashion industry. www.ethicalfashionforum.com.

Fibercrafts: Supplier of textile and dyeing supplies and books; also offers classes. www.fibercrafts.com.

Garthenor Organic Pure Wool: over 80 ecofriendly organic yarns, including from many rare breeds. www.organicpurewool.co.uk.

Green Fibres: a great site for eco-friendly yarns and fabrics. www.greenfibres.com.

Jenny Dean: the Web site of Master Natural Dyer and author of *Wild Color.* www.jennydean.co.uk/wordpress.

Local Wisdom: a fashion project recording the clothes-based ingenuity of communities. www.localwisdom.info.

London College of Fashion: center for sustainable fashion. www.fashion.arts.ac.uk/csf.htm.

Make Do & Mend: A crafty, green, information and design Web site trying to tackle the problems arising from the commercial direction of the fashion industry. www.make-do-and-mend.org.

Permaculture Association of Britain: Home of the UK Permaculture Network and Permaculture UK: www.permaculture.org.uk.

Prick Your Finger: offers classes, workshops, and exhibits in textile arts. www.prickyourfinger.com.

Plants for a Future: excellent database for finding and identifying useful plants. www.pfaf.org.

Real Seed Catalogue: a wonderful company based in Wales that has chosen to stay small and do what it loves, grow vegetable and herb seeds by hand for small garden use. Many are heirloom varieties and all are open-pollinated so you can save your own seed. No GMOs or F1 hybrids. www.realseeds.co.uk.

Renaissance Dyeing: workshops, fibers, and natural dye supplies. www.renaissancedyeing.com.

Royal Botanic Gardens, Kew: botanical education and biodiversity with a vast seed bank. You can even adopt a seed. *www.kew.org.*

Slow Food UK: regional resource for Slow Food International. *www.slowfood.org.uk.*

Super Naturale: an inspirational blog for "Craftivity, Frugality and Living, Home and Hearth." *www.supernaturale.com.*

Textiles Environment Design (TED): looks at the role that the designer can play in creating textiles that have a reduced impact on the environment and to provide a toolbox of designer-centered solutions. *www.tedresearch.net.*

UNITED STATES

Alpaca Association: everything you need to know about your local alpaca. *www.alpacainfo.com.*

Aurora Silk: an online source of natural dye supplies and mordants, as well as a direct importer of peace silk. *www.aurorasilk.com.*

California College of the Arts Textile Program: offers classes and degrees in textile arts. *www.cca.edu/academics/textiles.*

California Native Plant Society: goals of increasing understanding and appreciation of California's native plants and conserving them and their natural habitats through education, science, advocacy, horticulture, and land stewardship. *www.cnps.org.*

Center for Ecoliteracy: education for sustainable living. *www.ecoliteracy.org.*

Craigslist: a good Web site for finding and buying preowned cooking equipment for all your natural dyeing needs. *www.craigslist.org.*

Dharma Trading Company: a good basic supplier of natural dyes and mordants, as well as some nice fabrics ready for dyeing. *www.dharmatrading.com.*

Earth Hues: natural dyes for crafts and industry. *www.earthues.com.*

Freecycle Network: a good Web site for finding local free fabrics and dye equipment. *www.freecycle.org.*

Natural dye discussion groups on the Web: *www.groups.yahoo.com/group/NaturalDyes.*

Permacouture Institute: a nonprofit organization that supports regenerative design for textiles by offering classes, grassroots programs, and education on ecofashion and textiles. *www.permacouture.org.*

Project Laundry List: working on making air-drying laundry acceptable and desirable as a simple and effective way to save energy. *www.laundrylist.org.*

Sustainable Cotton Project: focuses on the production and use of cotton, one of the most widely grown and chemical-intensive crops in the world. *www.sustainablecotton.org.*

The Textile Arts Center: provides artists, students, and artisans with tools for making and sharing fiber art in a large, naturally lit workspace. *www.textileartscenter.com.*

University of California Berkeley, Botanical Garden: offers plant-based public education programs. *www.botanicalgarden.berkeley.edu.*

Yolo Wool Mill: processes scoured wool into finished products, including sliver, batting, roving, and various yarns. *www.yolowoolmill.com.*

PLANT RESOURCES

Heirloom Seeds: offers many types of pollinated heirloom seeds, nothing that is genetically modified. *www.heirloomseeds.com*.

Local Harvest: a source for finding locally grown produce and farm-grown fibers anywhere in the United States. *www.localharvest.org*.

Plants for a Future: a source for researching and learning more about plants that have edible, medicinal, and dye- and fiber-producing qualities. *www.pfaf.org*.

Seed Savers Exchange: a nonprofit group whose members have passed on approximately 1 million samples of rare garden seeds to other gardeners. *www.seedsavers.org*.

United Plant Savers: an organization whose mission is "to protect native medicinal plants of the United States and Canada and their native habitat while ensuring an abundant renewable supply of medicinal plants for generations to come." *www.unitedplantsavers.org*.

TEXTILE INSPIRATION

Adie + George: a story-filled bioregional fiber and local plant-dyed knitwear collaboration developed by me and my friend, designer Casey Larkin. *www.adieandgeorge.com*.

Danken: Hand-felted textiles made by Ashley Helvey, using organic local wool. *www.dankendanken.com*.

Ecco Eco: a wonderful, informative ecofashion, textile, and art blog by fiber artist Abigail Doan. *www.eccoeco.blogspot.com*.

Ecouterre: a fashion-forward Web site dedicated to the future of textiles and clothing. *www.ecouterre.com*.

India Flint: Australian textile and fiber artist India Flint creates botanical dyes for beautiful textiles. *www.indiaflint.com*.

Kate Fletcher: a great place to explore sustainable fashion and textiles. *www.katefletcher.com*.

Mr. Larkin: gorgeous designs with innovative fabrics and natural dyes, a labor of love from Casey Larkin. *www.mrlarkin.net*.

Selvedge: fine textiles from the gorgeous *Selvedge* textile magazine, Web site, and shop. Well worth a look. *www.selvedge.org*.

SLOW MOVEMENT INSPIRATION

Edible Schoolyard (ESY): "established in 1995, is a one-acre garden and kitchen classroom at Martin Luther King Jr. Middle School in Berkeley, California. It is a program of the Chez Panisse Foundation, a nonprofit organization founded by chef and author Alice Waters." *www.edibleschoolyard.org*.

Field Faring: social art projects that investigate the overlay of urban and rural systems upon the lives of specific communities. *www.fieldfaring.org*.

Forage Oakland: inspiration for finding neighborhood and urban sources for food (and dyes), as well as other useful plants. *www.forageoakland.blogspot.com*.

Mala'ai: the culinary garden of Waimea Middle School "Hands in the soil" health and wellness learning for students, families, and the larger community. *www.malaai.org*.

Non-Disposable Life: living a (beautiful!) year without packaging. *www.nondisposablelife.com*.

Slow Food International: the official site of the Slow Food movement. The organization states, "Slow Food brings together pleasure and responsibility, and makes them inseparable." *www.slowfood.com*.

Slow Lab: an inspiring collective of Slow experiments for art and life. *www.slowlab.net*.

FURTHER READING

Ashworth, Suzanne. 2002. *Seed to Seed: Seed Saving and Growing Techniques for Vegetable Gardeners*. 2nd ed. Decorah, Iowa: Seed Savers Exchange.

Barber, Elizabeth Wayland. 1991. *Prehistoric Textiles*. Princeton, New Jersey: Princeton University Press.

Barber, Elizabeth Wayland. 1994. *Women's Work: The First 20,000 Years. Women, Cloth, and Society in Early Times*. New York: W. W. Norton.

Barlow, Zenobia, and Michael Stone. 2005. *Ecological Literacy*. San Francisco, California: Sierra Club Books.

Benyus, Janine. 2002. *Biomimicry: Innovation Inspired by Nature*. New York: Perennial.

Black, Sandy. 2008. *Eco Chic: The Fashion Paradox*. London, England: Black Dog Publishing.

Buchanan, Rita. 1995. *A Dyer's Garden: From Plant to Pot. Growing Dyes for Natural Fibers*. Loveland, Colorado: Interweave Press.

Cardon, Dominique. 2007. *Natural Dyes: Sources, Tradition, Technology, and Science*. London, England: Archetype Publications.

Chanin, Natalie, and Stacie Stukin. 2008. *The Alabama Stitch Book: Projects and Stories Celebrating Hand-Sewing, Quilting and Embroidery for Contemporary Sustainable Style*. New York: STC Craft.

Colchester, Chloe. 2009. *Textiles Today: A Global Survey of Trends and Traditions*. London, England: Thames & Hudson.

Coyne, Kelly, and Erik Knutzen. 2008. *The Urban Homestead: Your Guide to Self-Sufficient Living in the Heart of the City*. Cambridge, Massachusetts: Process Publishing.

Crook, Jackie. 2007. *Natural Dyeing*. Asheville, North Carolina: Lark Books.

Dean, Jenny. 1994. *The Craft of Natural Dyeing*. Tunbridge Wells, England: Search Press.

Dean, Jenny, and Karen Diadick Casselman. 1999. *Wild Color: The Complete Guide to Making and Using Natural Dyes*. New York: Watson-Guptill.

Finlay, Victoria. 2002. *Color: A Natural History of the Palette*. New York: Random House.

Fletcher, Kate. 2008. *Sustainable Fashion and Textiles: A Design Journey*. London, England: Earthscan.

Flint, India. 2008. *Eco Colour: Environmentally Sustainable Dyes*. Sydney, Australia: Murdoch Books.

Fowler, Alys. 2009. *Garden Anywhere*. San Francisco: Chronicle Books.

Goldsmith, Sheherazads, and Alice Waters. 2007. *Slice of Organic Life*. New York: DK Publishing.

Goodwin, Jill. 2003. *A Dyer's Manual*. London, England: Ashman's.

Hoffman, Leslie, and Diane von Furstenburg. 2008. *FutureFashion White Papers*. New York: Earth Pledge.

Holmgren, David. 2002. *Permaculture: Principles and Pathways Beyond Sustainability*. Hepburn, Australia: Holmgren Design Services.

Lambert, Eva, and Tracy Kendall. 2010. *The Complete Guide to Natural Dyeing*. Loveland, Colorado: Interweave Press.

McDonough, William, and Michael Braungart. 2002. *Cradle to Cradle: Remaking the Way We Make Things*. New York: North Point Press.

McIntyre, Anne. 1997. *The Apothecary's Garden: How to Grow and Use Your Own Herbal Medicines*. London, England: Piatkus Books.

Petrini, Carlo. 2001. *Slow Food: Collected Thoughts on Taste, Tradition, and the Honest Pleasures of Food*. White River Junction, Vermont: Chelsea Green Publishing.

Rice, Miriam C., and Dorothy Beebee. 1980. *Mushrooms for Color*. Eureka, California: Mad River Press.

Rice, Mirian C., and Dorothy Beebee. 2007. *Mushrooms for Dyes, Paper, Pigments and Myco-Stix*. Forestville, California: Mushrooms for Color Press.

Richards, Lynne, and Ronald J. Tyrl. 2005. *Dyes from American Native Plants: A Practical Guide*. Portland, Oregon: Timber Press.

Rudkin, Linda. 2009. *Natural Dyes*. London, England: A&C Black.

Seiff, Joanne. 2009. *Knit Green: 20 Projects and Ideas for Sustainability*. Hoboken, New Jersey: Wiley.

Thayer, Samuel. 2010. *Nature's Garden: A Guide to Identifying, Harvesting and Preparing Edible Wild Plants*. Birchwood, Wisconsin: Forager's Harvest Press.

Wada, Yoshiko Iwamoto, Mary Kellogg Rice, and Jane Barton. 1999. *Shibori: The Inventive Art of Japanese Shaped Resist Dyeing*. Tokyo, Japan: Kodansha International.

Waters, Alice. 2007. *The Art of Simple Cooking: Notes, Lessons, and Recipes from a Delicious Revolution*. New York: Random House.

TRISTAN DAVISON

Tristan Davison: pages 11, 12, 13, 19, 21 above, 23 left, 26, 27, 30, 31 right, 32 above, 33 left and center, 35, 41, 43 below, 48, 50, 51 left and right, 60, 61, 62, 63, 64 left, 65 above, 75, 80 above left, 81, 83 below, 85, 86, 89, 90, 93, 102, 103, 105 above and below right, 106, 107 right, 109, 110, 111, 114 above and left, 115 above, 128 above left, 130, 140, 143 left

MARTHA DUERR

page 170

SCOTT FOSSEL

page 67 right

SARA LESLIE

pages 41, 77 center

MCCALLEN, MARIN

page 88

DEBRA MCCLINTON

pages 51 center, 65 below, 141 right

JUREE SONDKER

page 70 right

KATELYN TOTH-FEJEL

page 91

All other photographs are by the author.

INDEX

ACKNOWLEDGMENTS

This book could not have been possible without my family, friends, and community. My appreciation goes to so many. To Scott for his devoted mornings of motivation and love. Finnegan for being my natural-natural dyeing partner, and for being as fine with dyes as he is with food. Bergamot Eveny Fossel. My mom and dad for their nurture and nature, and for supplying such a deep creative well to be nourished from. Lissa, Cael, Kit, and Mo for kin inspiration and choosing such glamorous medieval careers. And all my grandparents. Juree Sondker, for her belief in giving this book life. The gorgeous photography and generosity of Tristan Davison. The beautiful photos of Marin McCallen. The talent and vibrant spirit of Debra McClinton and her shining images. The Waldorf training of Sarah Leslie, and for being an excellent assistant on the creation of this work. Thank you to Leslie Leslie for being their mom. Many thanks for the work of Marjorie Spock. Thank you to my colleagues and mentors in the textile program at the California College of the Arts for their continued enthusiastic support of Soil to Studio. Thank you to my students young and old for helping me to explore and cultivate color, especially to CCA students Ashley Brock, Aline Dargie, and Anabel Curry, Sadie Sturgeon, for their creative and sustainable natural dye projects, and Shoko Yamamuro and Erica Grossman for their hands-on help and research. Thank you to the U.C. Berkeley Botanical Garden for their love of plants, especially to Deepa Natarajan and Christine Manoux for their courageous creativity and collaboration. Thank you to the Edible Schoolyard, where many of these ideas were grown to harvest, especially to Amanda Rieux and Lissa Duerr. To the Trust for Conservation Innovation for their beloved support of Permacouture Institute. To Ashley Helvey for her felting expertise and love of sheep and weeds. To Leif Hendendal for the original Dinner to Dye For. Thank you to Abigail Doan for her kindred spirit; Mimi Robinson for bridging cultures through design; Dominque Leveuf for her aesthetic belief. So much appreciation and love to Lynda Grose and Kate Fletcher for being inspirational lights. Many immense thanks to Katelyn Toth-Fejel, for knowing the importance of bringing permaculture and fashion together, and for being an incredible support system. To Ms. Casey Larkin, tak always: thank you for your endless creativity, sense of humor, and fashion genius. And to Mobi, my trusty side dog, for sniffing out the good weeds from the bad and for being my enthusiastic foraging companion.

SASHA DUERR is an artist and designer who works with organic dyes and fibers, focusing on the creative reuse of materials. In her work, she is dedicated to a cross-pollination of textiles and environmental systems thinking, gaining inspiration from the ecological principles found in permaculture, as well as from regenerative design for food, clothing, and shelter.

In 2007, Sasha founded Permacouture Institute to encourage sustainable design and education in fashion and textiles from the ground up. Through Permacouture, Sasha has addressed audiences on natural dyes and sustainable textiles at colleges and universities across the country, and she consults on sustainable fashion for the fashion and textile industries. Sasha has received multiple grants to teach natural dyeing at the Edible Schoolyard in Berkeley, California, and has taught courses on Slow Textiles at artist workshops, colleges, and community and school garden programs. She serves on the panel of experts for the Nordic Initiative for Clean and Ethical.

Sasha's textile art and design has been shown in galleries and museums in the United States and abroad. Her work has been featured in publications such as San Francisco Magazine, Selvedge, Fast Company, and Eco Salon. Her bioregional knitwear collection with Casey Larkin is Adie + George. She teaches at the California College of the Arts, offering courses that focus on the convergence of ecoliteracy and social practice in textile art and design.